THE WOR  K

Getting the Job You Want

Fourth Edition

J. Michael Farr
Richard Gaither
R. Michael Pickrell

GLENCOE

Macmillan/McGraw-Hill

Lake Forest, Illinois   Columbus, Ohio   Mission Hills, California   Peoria, Illinois

Send all inquiries to:
GLENCOE DIVISION
Macmillan/McGraw-Hill
15319 Chatsworth Street
P.O. Box 9609
Mission Hills, CA 91346-9609

ISBN 0-02-668450-0

Printed in the United States of America.

11 12 13 14 15 16 17 18 19 20   DBH   99 98 97 96 95 94 93 92

CONTENTS

INTRODUCTION

. . . welcome to the chase

If you are out of work now or plan to look for a job in the near future, you are not alone. Each year over twenty million people in this country look for a job. Over half of all the people now working will have a different job within two years.

Very few of these millions of job-seekers have been trained in how to look for a job. Yet many of them say to themselves, *"I don't need anyone to show me how to find a job. I already know how to find a job."* Unfortunately, most of these job-seekers know far less than they think they know.

WHY MOST PEOPLE REMAIN UNEMPLOYED

One of the biggest barriers to a rewarding job-search is the belief in labor market myths. Many people base their job search on totally false information. Following are some common myths that often cause disastrous results:

Myth	Fact
Most interviewers are well trained.	Less than 5 percent receive professional training. You might have to take both parts — interviewer and interviewee.
Interviewers use only logic and reason.	Many rely on "gut reactions" since most applicants can't present their skills and don't know what the employer wants.
Employers consider only *paid* work experience.	Employers look for good attitude, education, and a desire to learn, even without experience.
There are no jobs.	*"Cop out!"* More and more small businesses are being started every year. More and more people are working every year.
Hard work, good education, and loyalty guarantee steady work.	Talk with hard-working, loyal, college graduates, out of work, and they'll say, *"There's only one guarantee for employment . . . learning how to look for a job!"*
All hiring begins at the personnel department.	This is true only for the untrained job-seeker. Most job openings are filled before they're listed. And many organizations don't even have a personnel department!
Most jobs are in *big* companies.	Definitely not true. Eighty percent of all work is done in small businesses. Ninety percent of all "first hires" occur in small businesses.

Employers won't talk to you unless they have an opening.	Wrong! Employers are always on the lookout for good workers. Be one!
Sending 1,000 resumes gets a job.	One good personal contact is worth 1,000 resumes.
There are good times and bad times to look for work.	Don't be trapped by this thought. While you are looking for work, *all the time is a good time for job-hunting.*

The average length of unemployment is from three to four months. Why does it take people so long to find work? Experience shows that people suffer from extended unemployment for one or more of the following reasons:

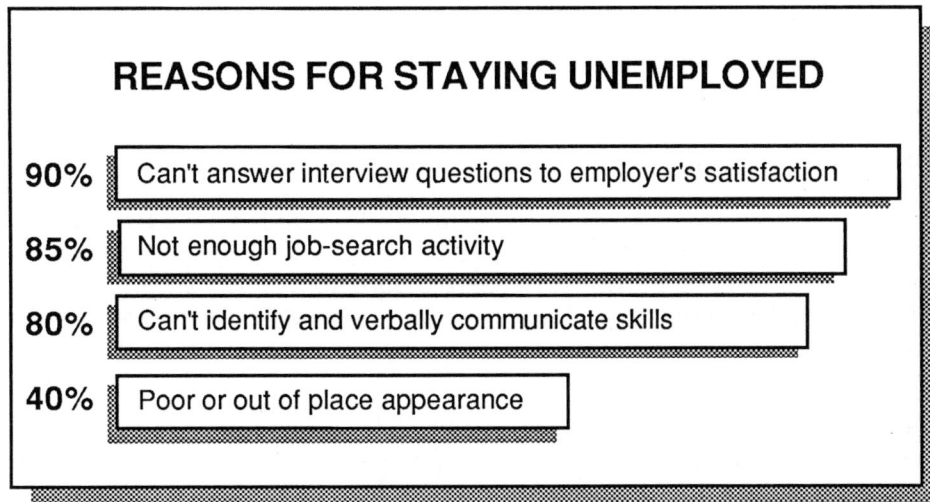

REASONS FOR STAYING UNEMPLOYED

90% Can't answer interview questions to employer's satisfaction

85% Not enough job-search activity

80% Can't identify and verbally communicate skills

40% Poor or out of place appearance

DESTRUCTIVE EFFECTS OF EXTENDED UNEMPLOYMENT

Some people feel that the world owes them a living. In one sense they're right. The world will give them a living. The problem is that it's not the type of living that people want to hang on to for very long.

Whether or not you decide to find work is your decision. But before you decide *not* to work, you should know that the price for extended unemployment is high, and you pay interest on that price for a lifetime. Here's what you can expect if you stay unemployed for a long period of time:

- depression
- low self-esteem
- lost friendships
- social isolation
- inability to accept rejection and help
- inability to finance a job-search
- lies and cheating
- anger and hostility
- mental illness
- physical illness

- poor appearance
- no money and no fun
- bill collectors
- welfare lines
- loss of action (becoming a "couch potato")
- physical abuse of other people
- rotten jobs
- bad relationships
- job skill loss
- drug abuse

WHAT *THE WORK BOOK* IS ALL ABOUT

Reducing the length of your unemployment by one or two weeks will help you avoid some of the depressing events described above. It can also mean lots of dollars in your pocket that would otherwise not be there. Increased happiness and more money — does that sound interesting? If so, you'll be extremely interested in *The Work Book*.

The development of *The Work Book* began with the authors' attempts to provide job-seekers with a proven, simple method for finding work in the shortest possible time, and with the least amount of anxiety and fear. To accomplish this the authors began by asking job-seekers and professional job-search trainers from all across this country for help. What advice did the authors receive?

● *"Keep it simple and brief."*

● *"Explain what to do and why."*

● *"Use lots of proven exercises."*

The result of this research is *The Work Book*, which is designed to meet two simple objectives:

1. **To decrease the amount of time you spend looking for work** once you actively begin your job-search. The average length of time for being unemployed *in a good economy* is fifteen to twenty weeks. You can do much better than that if you follow *The Work Book* plan.

2. **To eliminate much of the fear associated with looking for work and participating in an interview.** Since fear usually stems from a lack of knowledge and skill, *The Work Book* makes sure that you get a good dose of both.

The Work Book will teach you the skills you need to be more effective, efficient, and productive as a job-seeker. It will answer all five of the questions that job-seekers are most concerned about answering:

THE FIVE BASIC JOB-SEEKER QUESTIONS

1. Where are the jobs?

2. Whom do I talk to?

3. How do I contact these people?

4. What do I say when I contact them?

5. What's the easiest way to convince employers to hire me?

After reading and working through *The Work Book*, you will have no trouble answering these five questions. In fact, you will be among the 5 percent of the population who have been trained to be successful in their job-search. You will be able to

- meet the employer's expectations
- answer "hot" interview questions
- keep the interview focused on your skills
- create a job-search support network
- develop job leads
- design a JIST Card
- create resumes and cover letters

- discuss your achievements
- control your nervousness
- actively use the "hidden" job market
- write thank-you notes
- follow up after the interview
- watch your body language
- prove you are a good risk
- learn to use the phone for contacts

MOVING AHEAD

Before you begin reading and working your way through *The Work Book* — one word of caution. The authors tried their best to write a *magical job-search manual*. Unfortunately they failed. They were unable to develop the perfect, complete, easy answer for finding everyone his or her dream job instantly. They tried, but they just couldn't do it!

What this means to you is that you are going to have to do your fair share of the work. You will need to

1. **Identify a Realistic Job Objective or Career Goal** — You must know the type of work you want to get the maximum value from this book. Employers rarely hire people who want "anything" jobs.

2. **Take Some Risks, Talk with People** — People hire people! Quite simply, this means that you are going to have to take some interpersonal risks by meeting new people, recontacting "old" acquaintances, and talking with both former and potential employers. Everyone you used to know and everyone you will meet can be of help.

3. **Learn How the Labor Market and Hiring Process Work** — You must learn the rules of the game if you want to perform better in that game. *The Work Book* is geared toward teaching you how to look for work the smart way instead of looking for work the hard way.

4. **Invest the Time and Energy Needed to Make the Process Work** — If you learn nothing else from *The Work Book*, learn that your economic future is in your hands, and yours alone. No teacher, family member, friend, or counselor can guarantee your career success . . . it's up to you.

So now it's decision-making time. You need to decide whether or not the idea of a good living, nice home, emotional stability, strong family ties, and entertaining social life are worth the effort of doing the job-search right . . . the first time. If your answer is *"No, I don't want to waste the time,"* please give this book to someone who does want some of the nicer parts of life. If your answer is *"Yes,"* let's get started . . . right now!

1

EMPLOYER EXPECTATIONS

. . . measuring up

You cannot succeed in a job-search unless you first make some important decisions. Your decisions should answer two questions: *"What do I really want to do?"* and *"What can I do well?"* To answer these questions, think about your choices and abilities. Think long and hard before you decide.

Knowing what you want to do and can do well should give you a specific career goal, or job objective. Your goal should help you find a job that you will like. **You cannot do the work in this text without a career goal in mind.**[1] To be sure that you make good use of the text, write the title of the job you want below.

My Job Objective

Now that you are set on a goal, start thinking about what's on employers' minds. You must know what employers expect from good employees. This will help you convince employers that you are the right person for a certain job.

Knowing what to expect is one of the best ways to increase your job-seeking confidence and decrease your anxiety. By learning what to expect and how to meet these expectations, you'll be able to resolve a couple of serious problems:

Your problem — fear and nerves — These job-search enemies come from not knowing what to expect and a lack of practice.

Their problem — Inability to get good information from you during the interview.

---

[1]If you do not have a clear job objective, get help in defining one before going any further in this book.

An employer can choose only one person for any one position. From all the applicants, the employer will select the one who seems best qualified for the job. This person will be the one who most completely meets all of the employer's expectations for a good employee.

It is hard to learn the expectations of a certain employer before an interview. It is not hard, however, to learn the expectations of employers in general.

Try this exercise. Imagine that you are an employer. You are sitting behind a desk in your private office. You have been interviewing applicants for a position you need to fill. Your secretary is about to bring the next applicant into your office. How will you decide whether or not to hire this person? What clues will you look for? What will you expect from the person who best fits the job? Write at least ten of your expectations in the blanks below. Two examples have been provided to get you started.

good manners   _willing to learn_

_____   _____

_____   _____

_____   _____

_____   _____

Since you are playing the role of employer, there are no wrong answers in your list of expectations. As an employer you are free to exercise your personal preferences when choosing a new employee.

Different studies have shown, however, that most employers have **three major expectations.** With this in mind, choose the three expectations from your list that you think are the most important and write them on the lines below.

Expectation One:_____

Expectation Two:_____

Expectation Three: _____

In this chapter you will learn how you can use the three major employer expectations to both your and the employer's advantage. The exercises in the chapter will help you show employers how your life, work, and educational experiences match up to these expectations. Because employers rely heavily on interviewing when making their decisions, the emphasis in this chapter is on the interview and meeting the employer's needs and expectations.

EXPECTATION ONE: APPEARANCE

Do you look like the right person for the job?

You have probably heard of the importance of making a good first impression. Well, the impression you make in an interview is especially important. If you make a good first impression, the employer will consider you for the job. If you do not make a good first impression during an interview, your first impression will also be your last.

Even before you shake hands and introduce yourself, the employer begins forming an opinion of you. This is natural. Since you have little time to present yourself, your **appearance** greatly influences the employer's final opinion. This makes appearance one of the three main employer expectations.

Four aspects of your appearance concern employers. Employers are concerned about your appearance as shown by the way you **look, behave, write,** and **speak.** Each type of appearance is just as important as all of the others. If you meet these expectations, your first impression will be a good and lasting one.

The Way You Look

It may seem obvious, but good personal appearance and hygiene are extremely important when you are looking for a job. Many people suffering from extended unemployment stop paying attention to their physical selves. You should realize, however, that 40 percent of those remaining unemployed do so because of poor personal appearance. Don't be one of these people!

When you go to an interview, look like the right person for the job. In the first few seconds the employer will probably decide not to hire you if you have neglected your personal appearance. It makes no difference how skilled you are. The employer will usually hire someone with a pleasing appearance.

Three factors determine the way you look. These factors are **dress, grooming,** and **hygiene.**

Dress

The employer will notice immediately how you have dressed for the interview. Below are some basic rules to follow as you dress for an interview.

- Dress one step above what you would actually wear on the job. For example, if you would wear jeans and a T-shirt on the job, wear nice, casual clothes to the interview. You can find out what kind of clothing is worn on the job by visiting the company before the interview. Notice the dress of employees with jobs similar to the one you are seeking. If it is not possible to observe employees, use your good judgment. After a few interviews you will have a good idea how to adjust your dress to fit the situation.

- Never wear jeans, T-shirts, tennis shoes or other informal clothing to an interview. If you're applying for a job in which you would normally wear rough clothes, such as work boots, blue jeans, and sweatshirts, and you're worried about not looking like you're ready for work if you wear nicer clothes . . . don't worry. Just tell the interviewer that you've brought work clothes with you. By doing this you will meet the employer's expectation of good appearance, and you will still be ready for work.

- Wear clothes that are clean, neat, and in good condition. Buy good quality, well-fitted clothes and use them for interviews only.

- Dress conservatively! Do not wear loud colors or prints. Avoid mismatching colors and patterns (don't wear pink with orange or plaids with stripes). Avoid excessive or gaudy jewelry and accessories such as long necklaces with large medallions, and huge belt buckles. Shine your shoes. Match belts, purses, and other accessories with the rest of your clothes. If you feel that it's nobody's business but yours what type of clothes or styles you wear, don't expect to be hired right away. The price you pay for wearing the "in" style may be unemployment.

- Have a "dress rehearsal" before the interview. Dress exactly as you will for the interview, then ask a friend or relative for comments. *"I'm going to interview for a job as a* (fill in your job objective). *How do I look? Do I look like the right person for the job? Do you think I'm dressed one level above what other people doing this job would wear?"* Have your dress rehearsal in front of a mirror if there is no one to give helpful comments.

Now use your common sense and past experiences to decide how you would dress for a certain interview. Assume the interview is for a job that you want. How will you dress? Give the color and type of clothing for each category.

My Dressing Plan

Top: _____

_____

Bottom: _____

Shoes: _____

Socks: _____

Accessories (jewelry, ties, belts, etc.): _____

_____

Grooming

Grooming is another part of how you look. Follow the basic rules of good grooming listed below.

- Keep your hair well-groomed. It should be clean, combed, and neatly styled.

- Men, shave before you go to an interview. Mustaches and beards should be neatly combed and trimmed. If you want to grow a new mustache or beard, wait until after the interview. Mustaches and beards in their early stages do not look good.

- Neatly trim your fingernails.

- Use makeup, perfume, and after-shave sparingly.

Employers expect the right person for a job to be well-groomed. What does complete grooming include? Explain how you can make sure that you, personally, are well-groomed.

My Good Grooming Plan

Hair: _____

Face: _____

Hands: _____

Other: _____

_____

Hygiene

Hygiene is a third important factor in your personal appearance. Practice the following basic rules for good personal hygiene.

- Keep your body clean. Good personal hygiene begins with a clean body.
- Wash your hair regularly.
- Brush and floss your teeth every day.
- Use deodorants.
- Clean your fingernails.

Dress, grooming, and hygiene are closely related. Neglect of one hurts the others. Even if you are well-dressed and well-groomed, you will **not** have a good personal appearance if you have overlooked your hygiene.

Remember

Forty percent of the people who stay unemployed do so, in part, because their personal appearance does not meet employer expectations.[1]

The Way You Behave

Another part of appearance that employers consider is your **manner.** Manner refers to your personal behavior. How you behave in an interview gives the employer an idea of how you might behave on the job. Since you have little time to make an impression, your manner will greatly affect that impression.

Your manner during an interview should be natural and **positive.** Your manner will demonstrate good appearance if you conduct yourself with confidence. You should always show employers common courtesy. Do not, however, overdo your positive behavior. Just be yourself. Honesty and sincerity are also elements of a good manner.

The Way You Write

The third aspect of appearance is the paperwork that you must do to make your job-search successful. For example, almost all employers require applicants to fill out application forms. In later chapters you will learn to make and use various *paper tools* for your job-search. You must do your paperwork in a way that shows employers you are neat, complete, and accurate.

The Way You Speak

Another part of your appearance is the way you speak. Your manner of speaking is most important during the interview and during your phone contacts. Making a good appearance with your speaking means doing the following:

- thinking and organizing your thoughts before talking

---

[1]Janice Prazak and Robert A. Walker, *Job-Seeking Skills Reference Manual* (Minneapolis: MRC, 1971), p. 3.

- being open and frank with the interviewer
- showing enthusiasm in your speech
- talking about results, achievements, and how you can be of help to employers
- pronouncing words clearly
- using correct grammar

For whatever reasons, many employers like to hire people with good verbal communication skills. Be one of these people!

EXPECTATION TWO: DEPENDABILITY

Can you be counted on to do the job?

Employers hire people who show the most promise of being at work on time every day. Most companies operate on the idea that **time is money.** In turn, workers are usually paid for the amount of time they give the company. Employees who often miss work entirely, or frequently arrive late, cannot contribute fully. A highly skilled worker who is often absent will not produce as much as a more dependable worker with fewer skills. Nonproductive employees do not stay employed for long. Such workers often cost the company money rather than help it make a profit.

The second important employer expectation, then, is **dependability.** Dependability includes two specific qualities — **attendance** and **punctuality.** It also includes a general quality — **reliability.** During all parts of your job-search, you must convince employers that you can meet their expectations in these areas.

Attendance

Employers want to hire people who will maintain good attendance. Employers expect all workers to be on the job as scheduled. Employees who are at work every day produce more. In this way they make more money for the company — and for themselves.

During an interview your task is to give the interviewer specific and concrete examples of when and how you've shown good attendance in the past. You can do this with examples from any of your life, work, or educational experiences.

When you give employers **specific examples** of your skills, you show employers your ability to do good work. This also shows employers that you invested time and energy in preparing for your job-search and that you have the communication skills they want their workers to have. A specific example tells a story by describing some of the *who, what, where, when, why,* and *how* of that example. Remember the importance of using specific examples as you complete all of the exercises in *The Work Book.*

There are a few basic ways for you to show the employer during an interview that you meet his or her expectations of attendance. Show the employer that you've not missed many days at work or at school. If you did miss a few days and made up the work, say so! As a rule of thumb, six missed days a year, without serious illness, are considered acceptable to most employers . . . but not all.

You can reinforce your intention to maintain good attendance by showing employers your attendance records for team practices, club meetings, political activities, or volunteer activities. If you have won an award for attendance, make sure you tell employers. This would be the best possible method of demonstrating your attendance skills.

Now, identify three specific examples of your good attendance record.

Attendance example 1: _____

_____

Attendance example 2: _____

_____

Attendance example 3: _____

_____

Use your examples to prepare what you will say to the employer when the topic of attendance comes up in the interview. Here's a sample of the kind of statement you might make: *"I have a pattern of good attendance. I've not missed an appointment in over a year. I haven't missed a day of work in over six months, and my school attendance was approximately 95 percent."* Now write your statement in the space below.

My Attendance Statement

_____

_____

_____

_____

An unbelievable number of people miss their interviews due to a lapse of memory. Keep a written schedule of the date, time, location, and name of the interviewer. Missing the interview tells employers how little value you place on attendance and the job.

If you can't keep an appointment for an interview (problems with buses, the car, child care, etc.), call the employer before the interview. Explain the situation, take responsibility for the problem, and request another interview date. This is not a good situation, but it has happened to others. Your odds of saving the day are fifty-fifty.

Punctuality

Punctuality means being somewhere on time and completing your work on time. In the spaces below, describe specific situations in which you've demonstrated your punctuality. These examples will help you prove to the employer that you are a punctual person and a good employment risk. The following examples may help you get started:

- getting to work on time when there are difficult circumstances, such as bad weather or car problems.

- coming back from breaks and lunches on time

- not leaving work or school early

- meeting school or work assignment deadlines

- regularly arriving at meetings and appointments on time

- winning attendance awards at work, clubs, or school

Write three specific examples of how you have demonstrated punctuality.

Punctuality example 1: _____

_____

Punctuality example 2: _____

_____

Punctuality example 3: _____

_____

One of the easiest and most observable ways of showing your interest in punctuality is to show up for your interviews ten to fifteen minutes early. Don't arrive too early, however. A "too early" arrival may make the secretary and the interviewer uncomfortable. It may also tell the employer that you're "too hungry" for the position.

Now write a brief statement about your punctuality that might impress an interviewer. If you have a problem with punctuality, discuss the problem with your instructor or counselor and get started developing punctuality-related interview answers. Here's an example of what you might say: *"In all the time I was in school, I was never cited for being late for class. This carried over into my work and social life. I've even given up breakfast so that I wouldn't be late for work. I can't remember the last time I was late for an appointment."*

My Punctuality Statement (don't forget it!)

_____

_____

_____

Reliability

Excellent attendance and punctuality imply the more general employer expectation — **reliability.** Reliability means that the employer can count on you to do your job.

Compare yourself with the following descriptions of a reliable worker. Place a check (✔) next to each description of a reliable worker that you think describes you. If you have never had a job, think of these descriptions in terms of your educational, family, or life situations.

You are a reliable worker if you

____ put in an honest day's work each day.

____ learn something new at every opportunity.

____ get along with co-workers, customers, supervisors, and instructors.

____ leave your personal problems at home.

____ follow supervisory directions and company policies.

____ ask for a raise only after taking on more responsibility.

____ keep a clean, neat, safe workplace and take care of equipment.

____ ask for help, but only after you have tried your best to solve the problem.

____ admit to mistakes and work at improving your weaknesses.

____ work until the job is done right, even if it means unpaid overtime.

Select the three checked statements above that you feel most comfortable talking about. Give a brief, specific example of how each one applies to you.

Reliability example 1: _____

_____

Reliability example 2: _____

_____

Reliability example 3: _____

_____

Now write a short statement that you can use in interviews to show employers that you are a reliable worker. An example is the following statement: *"You'll find that I'm a reliable worker. On my last job I performed all of my cleaning duties well. Because of this, my boss asked me to be responsible for collecting the money from the pop machines. My tally was always on the mark. Later I was promoted to shift leader for the custodial crew."*

EXPECTATION THREE: SKILLS

What can you do?

Employers usually provide new employees with training for specific jobs. The training is designed to strengthen existing skills or teach new ones. In all cases, however, employers expect each person they hire to already have, or be able to develop, job skills. This means that you must have the potential to do the job and that you must express this potential in your job-seeking tools and during interviews.

Employers will ask about your skills during the interview. They can ask this question in many different ways. Common examples are

"What is your experience?"

"Why should I hire you?"

"What do you have to offer?"

"What do you know about the job?"

"How did you get your experience?"

"What do you think makes up a good worker in this field?"

Many job-seekers, such as the one in the following example, answer these questions vaguely:

Employer: *"What is your experience?"*

Job-seeker: *"Well, I was a secretary at Chrysler for three years and a bon-bon wrapper at Russell's Sweets for two years."*

This response does not describe the job-seeker's skills **specifically.** Instead, it mentions two job titles and two periods and places of employment. Compare this typical response to the one below.

Employer: *"Tell me about your experience."*

Job-seeker: *"I am interested in being a secretary in your music shop. I have three years' experience as a secretary at Chrysler. My skills include typing sixty words per minute accurately, good telephone presence, taking dictation, and training with all common office equipment. I can learn new procedures, filing systems, and so forth. My education includes a major in* *business prep in high school and an associate of arts degree from Yar-mouth Business College. I am dedicated to order and efficiency. In fact, I'm a secretary even when it comes to my hobby. I have a collection of over two thousand phonograph records. I have completely cataloged my collection with cross-indexes between musicians, songs, and composers. My love for music and attention to order seem to be natural extensions of my life experience. You see, my father was a librarian and my mother a musician. I learned much from them. I'm sure you will find my work for your company to be excellent."*

There is quite a difference between the two preceding examples. The first response barely answers the question; the second response is direct and complete. In this chapter you will learn how to make statements like the second job-seeker made.

When you answer interview questions about your skills, you must be specific and complete. To do this you must first learn about your own **skills triangle.** What is a skills triangle? A skills triangle is the grouping together of the three kinds of skills employers are looking for in employees. Everyone has a skills triangle, but most people don't know how to use it to find work. You will soon be one of the few job-seekers who does know how to use the skills triangle.

Whether the employers know it or not, during an interview they want you to talk about three types of skills: **job-related skills, self-management skills,** and **transferable skills.** These three types of skills make up your own personal triangle of skills. By identifying your personal skills triangle you can become a confident and effective job-seeker. You can then meet the employer's expectation for skills and show the employer that you are a well-rounded individual who will be an excellent worker.

Your Skills Triangle

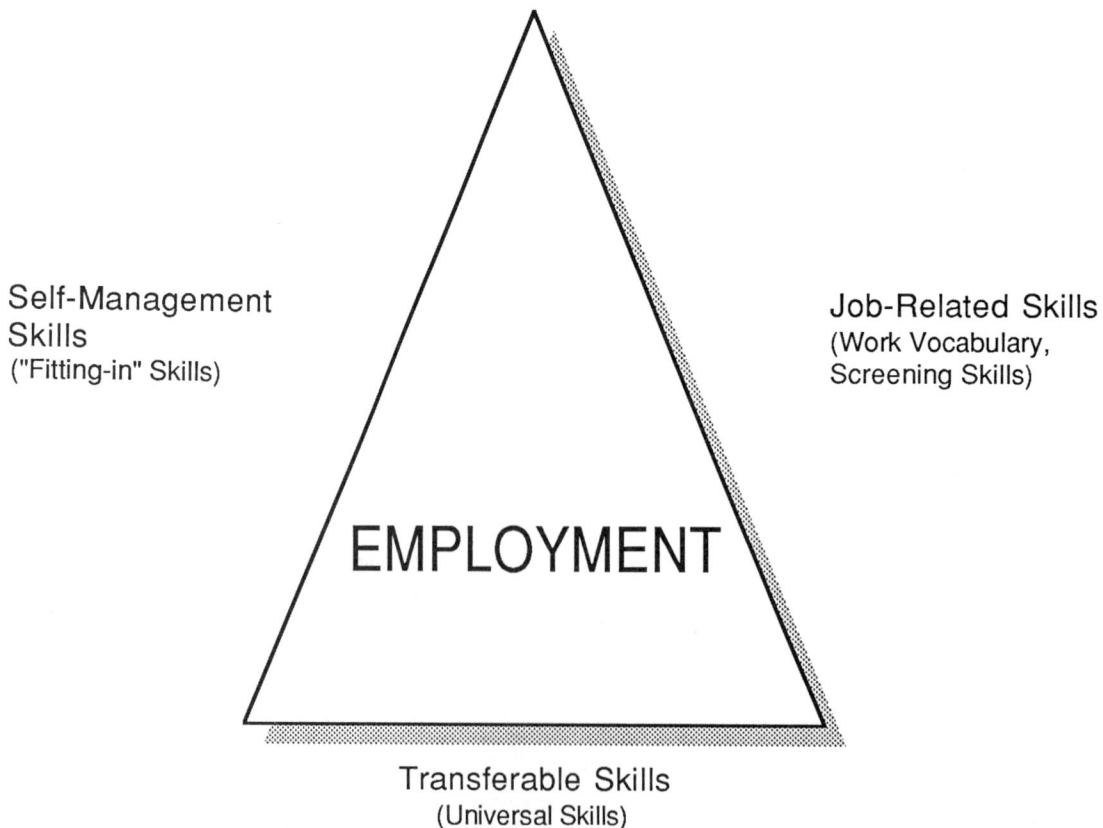

Self-Management Skills ("Fitting-in" Skills)

Job-Related Skills (Work Vocabulary, Screening Skills)

EMPLOYMENT

Transferable Skills (Universal Skills)

Every part of your job-search is affected by the ways in which you identify and present your skills.

The following exercises in this chapter will help you identify and list the skills in your personal skills triangle. In the next chapter you will identify your abilities and experiences in such areas as education, hobbies, and personal successes. After completing these two chapters, you will have lists of **specific** skills and experiences in each of the following categories:

Job-related Skills	Work Experience	Leisure Activities
Transferable Skills	Education and Training	Life Experiences
Self-management Skills	Interests and Hobbies	Successes/Achievements

As you develop your lists of skills, make sure that your responses relate to the job you want. In this way you can determine your potential to do that particular job.

Your Job Objective

As a reminder from page 8, your job objective is _____

_____ .

You are now ready to begin making a list of your skills that relate to this job objective.

Job-Related Skills

Job-related skills are the basic work skills needed to do a good job. Employers ask about job-related skills during the interview so that they can determine whether or not applicants have a working knowledge of the job.

Job-related skills are discussed using the words or vocabulary of the particular field of work. For example, carpenters *"set rafters,"* do *"trim work,"* *"hang joists,"* and use *"stringers"* for stairs. These words would not normally fit in the vocabulary of a secretary, who would be expected to *"word process,"* *"take shorthand,"* *"schedule appointments,"* and *"keep files."*

Sometimes job-related skills are called **screening skills** because they screen out applicants who are unable to show the employer that they understand the demands of the job. You should realize that when employers ask you about your experiences, they want to know if you have the basic knowledge and skills to do the job.

Regardless of the type of work you want, all job-related skills fall into four simple categories: **data, people, things,** and **ideas.** It's easier to talk about your job-related skills if you think about them as being broken down into these categories.

Data

The category of data involves working with facts, numbers, and other pieces of information. What type of information will you be responsible for in your new job? Some examples are customer files, expense reports, recordkeeping, and schedules. List the kinds of information you will work with in the job you are seeking.

1. _____	5. _____	9. _____
2. _____	6. _____	10. _____
3. _____	7. _____	11. _____
4. _____	8. _____	12. _____

People

The category of people involves working with people in different ways. What types of involvement will you have with other people in doing your job? Some examples are meeting customers, handling complaints, counseling children, and supervising others. List the ways in which you will work with people.

1. _____   5. _____   9. _____

2. _____   6. _____   10. _____

3. _____   7. _____   11. _____

4. _____   8. _____   12. _____

Things

The category of things involves working with tools, machines, or equipment. What tools, machines, or equipment will you probably have to operate on your next job? Some examples are typewriter, word processor, ohm meter, tape recorder, arc welder, and saw. List the tools, machines, or pieces of equipment that you will probably operate.

1. _____   5. _____   9. _____

2. _____   6. _____   10. _____

3. _____   7. _____   11. _____

4. _____   8. _____   12. _____

Ideas

The category of ideas is involved with creativity. What types of ideas will you need to use in doing a good job? Some examples are promotional ideas, organizing inventory, solving problems, and being inventive. List the ways in which you will use ideas in your job.

1. _____   5. _____   9. _____

2. _____   6. _____   10. _____

3. _____   7. _____   11. _____

4. _____   8. _____   12. _____

Summarizing Your Job-Related Skills

Now go back and circle every item in each of the four categories with which you have had actual or related experience. This experience can come from your life, work, or education.

Use your circled information to write statements about your job-related skills in the space provided on the next page. Then list examples from your own experiences that support your statement. Also explain the connection between your experience and the job you want. The following sample of a job-related skills statement will help you get started.

"I can operate a Wang word processor (things), *take dictation at 120 wpm, and was responsible for over forty customer accounts* (data). *I also trained and supervised a crew of five in a fast-food restaurant* (people) *and had to develop a new inventory system to cut down waste* (ideas)."

Job-Related Skills

Statement: _____

_____

Example: _____

_____

_____

Connection: _____

_____

_____

Job-Related Skills

Statement: _____

_____

Example: _____

_____

_____

Connection: _____

_____

_____

Job-Related Skills

Statement: _____

_____

Example: _____

_____

_____

Connection: _____

_____

_____

Transferable Skills

Unlike job-related skills, which tend to be used only in one type of work, transferable skills are skills that can be used in every occupation, regardless of the type of work. They are **universal** skills — you can transfer them from one type of work to another without much effort on your part or training from the employer.

Many employers think that if you are able to use a skill in one situation, you should be able to use that skill in another job, even if the work appears to be unrelated to your past employment or educational experience. For this reason, your transferable skills are often more important than your job-related skills. This is especially true if you are changing careers or making the transition from school to work.

Suppose that an automobile mechanic wants a job repairing household appliances. The mechanic should emphasize general mechanical skills, not specific automotive skills. The household appliance employer will be interested in the mechanic's general skills: Can the mechanic use hand tools? Can the mechanic troubleshoot, repair, adjust, and maintain mechanical devices? The employer does not care that the mechanic can pull a 1963 Chevrolet engine. The employer is not interested in knowing that the mechanic can grind pistons, rebuild carburetors, and adjust ignition timing.

In identifying your transferable skills, do not overlook the skills you've gained from everyday living. Most job-seekers fail to see this potential. These skills can, however, help you meet an employer's expectations.

If you do not already know your transferable skills, complete the transferable skills exercise on pages 23 and 24. This exercise will help you identify at least ten of your transferable skills.

Once you've identified your transferable skills, you need to develop them into statements that you can make in an interview, which will show employers that you are the best person for the job. Below are some sample statements about transferable skills. Each statement is followed by an example and a connection to a specific job.

Transferable skill statement: *"I can meet deadlines."*

Example: *"While in school, I rarely missed a due date on an assignment."*

Connection: *"If I was able to meet deadlines in school, I will also be able to meet your work deadlines and quotas."*

Transferable skill statement: *"I can keep financial records."*

Example: *"As a full-time homemaker I handled all of the family money, including savings and checking, without ever bouncing a check or failing to pay a bill on time."*

Connection: *"If I could handle the family finances so well for twenty years, while taking care of all of the other household chores at the same time, I could be a good account clerk for you."*

Transferable skill statement: *"I'm a well-organized person."*

Example: *"At my last job I had six bosses. I had to organize my time and set priorities to get the job done to everyone's satisfaction."*

Connection: *"If I could handle that confusion, I'm sure I'll be able to deal with the organizational demands of this job."*

Transferable skill statement: *"I'm a good explainer."*

Example: *"Whenever anyone at work had trouble understanding a procedure, they came to me for an explanation."*

Connection: *"I can learn quickly, train new workers, and help others."*

Now choose the three transferable skills from your list that you think will most interest potential employers. Write these skills as complete statements on page 25. Then include examples from your own experiences that support your statements. Also state the connection between each ability and the job you want.

Transferable Skills Checklist

Review this list of transferable skills and check ✓ all of the skills that you feel are skills you have. Check the **EDUCATION** column if you acquired that skill during your education or through a training program. Check the **LIFE** column if you acquired the skill anywhere else, which would include paid employment, volunteer activities, and general life experience. Check the third column, **NEXT JOB**, if you feel you will need that skill in the next job you have that meets your primary job objective.

EDUCATION	LIFE	NEXT JOB		EDUCATION	LIFE	NEXT JOB		EDUCATION	LIFE	NEXT JOB	
☐	☐	☐	act/perform	☐	☐	☐	copy information	☐	☐	☐	gather information
☐	☐	☐	adapt to situations	☐	☐	☐	correspond w/others	☐	☐	☐	gather materials
☐	☐	☐	advise people	☐	☐	☐	create	☐	☐	☐	generate
☐	☐	☐	analyze data	☐	☐	☐	delegate	☐	☐	☐	guide/lead
☐	☐	☐	anticipate problems	☐	☐	☐	deliver	☐	☐	☐	handle complaints
☐	☐	☐	appraise service	☐	☐	☐	demonstrate	☐	☐	☐	handle equipemnt
☐	☐	☐	arrange functions	☐	☐	☐	design	☐	☐	☐	handle money
☐	☐	☐	assemble products	☐	☐	☐	detail	☐	☐	☐	help people
☐	☐	☐	assess situations	☐	☐	☐	detect	☐	☐	☐	illustrate
☐	☐	☐	audit records	☐	☐	☐	determine	☐	☐	☐	imagine solutions
☐	☐	☐	bargain/barter	☐	☐	☐	develop	☐	☐	☐	implement
☐	☐	☐	be cost conscious	☐	☐	☐	direct others	☐	☐	☐	improve
☐	☐	☐	be responsible for	☐	☐	☐	dispense information	☐	☐	☐	improvise
☐	☐	☐	budget money	☐	☐	☐	distribute	☐	☐	☐	inform people
☐	☐	☐	build	☐	☐	☐	do precision work	☐	☐	☐	initiate actions
☐	☐	☐	buy products/services	☐	☐	☐	do public relations work	☐	☐	☐	inspect products
☐	☐	☐	calculate numbers	☐	☐	☐	draft	☐	☐	☐	install
☐	☐	☐	chart information	☐	☐	☐	drive	☐	☐	☐	instruct
☐	☐	☐	check for accuracy	☐	☐	☐	edit	☐	☐	☐	interpret data
☐	☐	☐	classify information	☐	☐	☐	encourage	☐	☐	☐	interview people
☐	☐	☐	collect money	☐	☐	☐	endure long hours	☐	☐	☐	invent
☐	☐	☐	communicate	☐	☐	☐	enforce	☐	☐	☐	inventory
☐	☐	☐	compare data	☐	☐	☐	entertain	☐	☐	☐	investigate
☐	☐	☐	compile statistics	☐	☐	☐	establish	☐	☐	☐	lead people
☐	☐	☐	compute data	☐	☐	☐	estimate	☐	☐	☐	learn
☐	☐	☐	conceptualize	☐	☐	☐	evaluate	☐	☐	☐	learn quickly
☐	☐	☐	conduct	☐	☐	☐	examine	☐	☐	☐	liaise
☐	☐	☐	confront others	☐	☐	☐	exchange	☐	☐	☐	lift (heavy)
☐	☐	☐	construct buildings	☐	☐	☐	exhibit	☐	☐	☐	lift (moderate)
☐	☐	☐	consult w/others	☐	☐	☐	expand	☐	☐	☐	listen
☐	☐	☐	contact others	☐	☐	☐	expedite	☐	☐	☐	locate information
☐	☐	☐	contact w/others	☐	☐	☐	explain	☐	☐	☐	log information
☐	☐	☐	control costs	☐	☐	☐	explore	☐	☐	☐	make/create
☐	☐	☐	control people	☐	☐	☐	file records	☐	☐	☐	make decisions
☐	☐	☐	control situations	☐	☐	☐	find information	☐	☐	☐	make policy
☐	☐	☐	converse w/others	☐	☐	☐	fix/repair	☐	☐	☐	manage a business
☐	☐	☐	coordinate activities	☐	☐	☐	follow directions	☐	☐	☐	manage people
☐	☐	☐	cope w/deadlines	☐	☐	☐	follow through	☐	☐	☐	measure boundaries

Transferable Skills Checklist
(continued)

EDUCATION	LIFE	NEXT JOB	
☐	☐	☐	mediate problems
☐	☐	☐	meet the public
☐	☐	☐	memorize information
☐	☐	☐	mentor others
☐	☐	☐	monitor progress
☐	☐	☐	motivate others
☐	☐	☐	move materials
☐	☐	☐	negotiate
☐	☐	☐	nurse
☐	☐	☐	nurture
☐	☐	☐	observe
☐	☐	☐	obtain
☐	☐	☐	operate equipment
☐	☐	☐	order goods/supplies
☐	☐	☐	organize data
☐	☐	☐	organize people
☐	☐	☐	organize tasks
☐	☐	☐	own/operate business
☐	☐	☐	paint
☐	☐	☐	perceive needs
☐	☐	☐	perform routine work
☐	☐	☐	persuade others
☐	☐	☐	plan
☐	☐	☐	plant
☐	☐	☐	prepare materials
☐	☐	☐	print
☐	☐	☐	process information
☐	☐	☐	process materials
☐	☐	☐	produce
☐	☐	☐	program
☐	☐	☐	promote
☐	☐	☐	protect property
☐	☐	☐	provide maintenance
☐	☐	☐	question others
☐	☐	☐	raise money
☐	☐	☐	read reference books
☐	☐	☐	recommend
☐	☐	☐	record data

EDUCATION	LIFE	NEXT JOB	
☐	☐	☐	recruit people
☐	☐	☐	rectify
☐	☐	☐	reduce costs
☐	☐	☐	refer people
☐	☐	☐	rehabilitate people
☐	☐	☐	remember information
☐	☐	☐	remove
☐	☐	☐	repair
☐	☐	☐	replace
☐	☐	☐	report information
☐	☐	☐	research
☐	☐	☐	resolve problems
☐	☐	☐	restore
☐	☐	☐	retrieve information
☐	☐	☐	review
☐	☐	☐	run meetings
☐	☐	☐	schedule
☐	☐	☐	seek out
☐	☐	☐	select
☐	☐	☐	sell
☐	☐	☐	separate
☐	☐	☐	sequence
☐	☐	☐	service customers
☐	☐	☐	service equipment
☐	☐	☐	set goals/objectives
☐	☐	☐	set up equipment
☐	☐	☐	set up systems
☐	☐	☐	sew
☐	☐	☐	shape
☐	☐	☐	signal
☐	☐	☐	size up situations
☐	☐	☐	sketch
☐	☐	☐	socialize
☐	☐	☐	solve problems
☐	☐	☐	sort
☐	☐	☐	speak in public
☐	☐	☐	study
☐	☐	☐	supervise

EDUCATION	LIFE	NEXT JOB	
☐	☐	☐	supply
☐	☐	☐	support
☐	☐	☐	survey
☐	☐	☐	synthesize
☐	☐	☐	tabulate
☐	☐	☐	take instructions
☐	☐	☐	tend equipment
☐	☐	☐	test
☐	☐	☐	think ahead
☐	☐	☐	think logically
☐	☐	☐	tolerate interruptions
☐	☐	☐	track
☐	☐	☐	train/teach
☐	☐	☐	transcribe
☐	☐	☐	transfer
☐	☐	☐	translate
☐	☐	☐	travel
☐	☐	☐	treat
☐	☐	☐	troubleshoot
☐	☐	☐	tutor
☐	☐	☐	type
☐	☐	☐	understand
☐	☐	☐	unite people
☐	☐	☐	update information
☐	☐	☐	upgrade
☐	☐	☐	use hand/eye coordination
☐	☐	☐	use words correctly
☐	☐	☐	verify
☐	☐	☐	visit
☐	☐	☐	visualize
☐	☐	☐	volunteer
☐	☐	☐	weigh
☐	☐	☐	work quickly
☐	☐	☐	write procedures
☐	☐	☐	write promo material
☐	☐	☐	write proposals
☐	☐	☐	write reports
☐	☐	☐	write technical work

Transferable Skills

Statement: _____

_____

Example: _____

_____

_____

Connection: _____

_____

_____

Transferable Skills

Statement: _____

_____

Example: _____

_____

_____

Connection: _____

_____

_____

Transferable Skills

Statement: _____

_____

Example: _____

_____

_____

Connection: _____

_____

_____

Self-Management Skills

Self-management skills make up the last part of your skills triangle. These skills tell the employer whether or not your personality fits the personality of the company, the bosses, and the co-workers. Over 50 percent of the people who are **not** successful on the job have trouble with their co-workers and bosses, so it's important for you to show employers how you fit into their operations. Many employers would rather hire an inexperienced worker with good self-management skills than an experienced worker who might cause problems.

If you are not sure what self-management skills you have, do the exercise on page 27. This exercise will help you identify your strongest self-management skills.

Now select two of your strongest self-management skills and write these as complete statements. Then include examples from your own experiences that support your statements. Also show a connection between each skill and the job you want.

Self-Management Skills

Statement: _____

_____

Example: _____

_____

_____

Connection: _____

_____

_____

Self-Management Skills

Statement: _____

_____

Example: _____

_____

_____

Connection: _____

_____

_____

Self-Management Skills Checklist

Review this list of self-management skills and check any 3 that you believe you exhibit over 50% of the time. Place a second check next to the ten skills that you believe would be most important in the next job you have that meets your primary job objective.

I EXHIBIT	NEXT JOB		I EXHIBIT	NEXT JOB		I EXHIBIT	NEXT JOB	
☐	☐	academic	☐	☐	active	☐	☐	accurate
☐	☐	adaptable	☐	☐	adventurous	☐	☐	affectionate
☐	☐	aggressive	☐	☐	alert	☐	☐	ambitious
☐	☐	artistic	☐	☐	assertive	☐	☐	attractive
☐	☐	bold	☐	☐	broad-minded	☐	☐	businesslike
☐	☐	calm	☐	☐	careful	☐	☐	cautious
☐	☐	charming	☐	☐	cheerful	☐	☐	clear-thinking
☐	☐	clever	☐	☐	competent	☐	☐	competitive
☐	☐	confident	☐	☐	conscientious	☐	☐	conservative
☐	☐	considerate	☐	☐	cool	☐	☐	cooperative
☐	☐	courageous	☐	☐	creative	☐	☐	curious
☐	☐	daring	☐	☐	deliberate	☐	☐	democratic
☐	☐	dependable	☐	☐	determined	☐	☐	dignified
☐	☐	discreet	☐	☐	dominant	☐	☐	eager
☐	☐	easygoing	☐	☐	efficient	☐	☐	emotional
☐	☐	energetic	☐	☐	enterprising	☐	☐	enthusiastic
☐	☐	fair-minded	☐	☐	farsighted	☐	☐	firm
☐	☐	flexible	☐	☐	forceful	☐	☐	formal
☐	☐	frank	☐	☐	friendly	☐	☐	generous
☐	☐	gentle	☐	☐	good-natured	☐	☐	healthy
☐	☐	helpful	☐	☐	honest	☐	☐	humorous
☐	☐	idealistic	☐	☐	imaginative	☐	☐	independent
☐	☐	individualistic	☐	☐	industrious	☐	☐	informal
☐	☐	ingenious	☐	☐	intellectual	☐	☐	intelligent
☐	☐	intentive	☐	☐	kind	☐	☐	leisurely
☐	☐	lighthearted	☐	☐	likable	☐	☐	logical
☐	☐	loyal	☐	☐	mature	☐	☐	methodical
☐	☐	meticulous	☐	☐	mild	☐	☐	moderate
☐	☐	modest	☐	☐	natural	☐	☐	obliging
☐	☐	open-minded	☐	☐	opportunistic	☐	☐	optimistic
☐	☐	organized	☐	☐	original	☐	☐	outgoing
☐	☐	painstaking	☐	☐	patient	☐	☐	peaceable
☐	☐	persevering	☐	☐	pleasant	☐	☐	poised
☐	☐	polite	☐	☐	practical	☐	☐	precise
☐	☐	progressive	☐	☐	prudent	☐	☐	purposeful
☐	☐	pressure resistant	☐	☐	punctual	☐	☐	productive
☐	☐	quick	☐	☐	quiet	☐	☐	rational
☐	☐	realistic	☐	☐	reasonable	☐	☐	reflective
☐	☐	relaxed	☐	☐	reliable	☐	☐	reserved
☐	☐	resourceful	☐	☐	responsible	☐	☐	retiring
☐	☐	robust	☐	☐	self-confident	☐	☐	sensible
☐	☐	sensitive	☐	☐	serious	☐	☐	sharp-witted
☐	☐	sincere	☐	☐	sociable	☐	☐	spontaneous
☐	☐	spunky	☐	☐	stable	☐	☐	steady
☐	☐	strong	☐	☐	strong-minded	☐	☐	sympathetic
☐	☐	tactful	☐	☐	teachable	☐	☐	tenacious
☐	☐	thorough	☐	☐	thoughtful	☐	☐	tolerant
☐	☐	tough	☐	☐	trusting	☐	☐	trustworthy
☐	☐	unaffected	☐	☐	unassuming	☐	☐	understanding
☐	☐	unexcitable	☐	☐	uninhibited	☐	☐	verbal
☐	☐	versatile	☐	☐	warm	☐	☐	wholesome
☐	☐	wise	☐	☐	witty	☐	☐	zany

OK. ANSWER **THIS** ONE! WHAT WORK WERE YOU DOING ON SEPTEMBER 6, 1981... LATE AFTERNOON... JUST BEFORE QUITTING TIME?!

I WAS WORKING AS A CUSTODIAN AT CITY HALL. I WAS WASHING THE THIRD-FLOOR WINDOWS THAT DAY AND HURRYING TO FINISH SO THAT...

THE DATATRAKT
... knowledge is power

A well-known philosopher once said, *"Knowledge is power!"* After completing Chapter 1, you should see that knowledge really does give you power. In that chapter you increased both your knowledge and power by doing the following:

- learning that an employer's three main expectations are **appearance, dependability, and skills.**

- beginning to build your own skills triangle of **transferable skills, job-related skills, and self-management skills.**

- starting to compare and **connect** your life, work, and educational experiences to the expectations of the employer.

- learning the importance of giving **specific examples** of how you use your skills and experiences.

In gaining this knowledge you probably have had some trouble remembering "specifics" about your skills and experiences. In fact, you even may have already suffered some "memory loss" about what you learned in Chapter 1. This brings us to a serious problem for most job-seekers — **poor memory.**

Too many job-seekers rely on memory rather than written notes. Memory alone is not enough. You must write down information about your former employers, references, dates, phone numbers, addresses, and much more. Nothing makes a worse impression than forgetting "simple" information in an interview. And this type of information is easy to forget.

If you find this hard to believe, here's a little memory quiz.

- Have you ever forgotten a phone number, address, or zip code?

- Have you ever forgotten test answers — which you knew yesterday?

- Have you ever forgotten the names of people you have just met?

- Can you recite the phone numbers, addresses, and zip codes of your former employers and references?

If you still don't believe that your poor memory is your enemy, read the following number and address — **only one time** — and then try to repeat it accurately.

1-490-876-3982
2175 N. Highland Blvd.
San Francisco, CA 93120

If you had difficulty with this no-stress exercise, just think how much trouble you will have trying to remember information during the heat of the interview.

Remember
Ninety percent of the people suffering from extended unemployment can't remember enough about themselves to answer interview questions, and 80 percent have trouble identifying and discussing their skills.

Unlike the untrained job-seeker, you can overcome the memory problem by keeping track of your job-search data. You can accomplish this by using the *DataTrakt* booklet attached to the last page of this book.

Turn to the back of the book and tear out your *DataTrakt*. You will enter all the information in this chapter's exercises into your own *DataTrakt*.

Your *DataTrakt* will provide you with a foundation for sensible job-seeking. Your *DataTrakt* will be an organized record of the information employers want to know. Your education, work history, and other important information will all be included.

By completing your *DataTrakt* completely, neatly, and as accurately as possible, you will meet the employer's expectations of

- **Appearance** — You'll have no scratch outs, deletions, or mistakes on applications. Attractive paperwork does count in your favor!

- **Dependability** — Your preparation will show the employer that you've "done more than expected" to get the job — a good first impression.

- **Skills** — When you use the information in your *DataTrakt*, you will show employers how your life, work, and educational experiences match the demands of the job.

In later chapters you will learn to use other job-search tools. These include the job application, JIST Card, resume, telephone contact, and interview. Each will be based on the information in your personal *DataTrakt*. Take special care in making your *DataTrakt*. It will save you time and effort later.

MAKING YOUR DATATRAKT

Before assembling your *DataTrakt*, find a quiet place to work. Have handy the personal records that you have saved over the years. You should have access to a telephone and a phone book since you may need to gather more data. Use a pencil and get a good no-mark eraser so you can make corrections. When you have a place to work and the recommended supplies, you may continue.

Your job-search will require a great deal of personal information. Different employers ask for different bits of information, but most of your information will be of interest to every employer. The following list outlines the general areas of personal data commonly required by employers.

- Personal identification
- Work experience
- Education and training
- Job-related personal information
- References

As you read each section in this chapter, **print** your data in the spaces provided in your own *DataTrakt*. When an item does not relate to you, put a dash (—) in the appropriate blank. If any section poses a problem, or if you believe one of your answers might create a negative impression on the employer, you must do three things:

1. Leave that answer blank until you get help and feel comfortable with your response. **Never write anything negative in your *DataTrakt*!**

2. Turn to the same section in the application chapter to see if the problem is addressed there.

3. Ask for help from your instructor.

Personal Identification

The first section of your *DataTrakt* is entitled *Personal Identification*. This section will contain your basic personal data. Read the following instructions and **print** the data in your *DataTrakt*.

Name

Print your **complete** name (first, middle, last).

Social Security Number

Print your social security number. Be sure the number is correct. If you do not have a social security number, apply for one now. Go to the nearest social security office or local post office.

Present Address

Print your present address. List your street address, RFD or box number, city, state, and zip code. Many applications will ask, *"How long have you lived at this address?"* Your response may show the employer that you are stable and reliable. Print the length of time you have lived at your present address.

Previous Address

Print your previous address and the length of time you lived at that address. As with your present address, your response can show employers that you are stable and dependable.

Telephone Number

Print your home phone number. Also print the number of another phone (the number of a friend or relative, for example) where you may be reached. First list your area code. Then list the number. If you do not have a home phone, list the number of a reliable friend or relative who can take your messages. Be sure this person knows that potential employers may be calling. It is wise to list **two** numbers. Then an employer can reach you even if no one answers the first phone.

Physical Characteristics

Print your physical characteristics. These include your height, weight, eye color, and hair color. Just as some jobs require strength and reaching ability, others require certain heights and weights.

Birth Information

Give the date and place of your birth. Give the correct information — it is illegal for employers to discriminate because of age.

Citizenship

Check the appropriate space if you are a United States citizen. If you are not a citizen, list your visa number and explain the type of visa you have.

Marital Status

Print either *married* or *single*. As with age, it is illegal for employers to discriminate against you based on your marital status.

Emergency Information

Print your data about whom to notify in an emergency. List that person's name, relationship to you, home address, home phone, work address, and work phone.

Medical Information

Print the name, address, and phone number of your physician. Also print the date of your most recent physical exam. Some applications require this information. If you do not remember the date of your last exam, check with your doctor, who has the date on file. Many employers require a recent physical exam. If you are restricted in the type of work you can do, are taking medications that might affect your ability to do the job, or are under a doctor's care, consider your responses carefully before entering any information into your booklet.

Work Experience

Basically, *work experience* refers to specific data about past jobs. This information includes the names of former employers and the period of employment for each job. It also includes the titles of positions held and the skills required to do the job.

The work-experience section is one of the most important parts of your *DataTrakt*. In this section you will record the many skills, abilities, and experiences you have to offer by analyzing and evaluating each of your past work experiences.

There are three kinds of work experience: paid, unpaid (volunteer), and military. You will want to define these areas clearly so you can show employers how you will meet their major expectations.

Take extra care in preparing the work-experience sections of your *DataTrakt*. Your job-search will depend heavily on this information. You will learn later how to emphasize other qualifications if you do not have much work experience.

You must be especially careful to list accurate and complete information in this section. You may need to dig through your personal records. You also may need to thumb through the phone book or call directory assistance. You should ask former employers for any data you have difficulty remembering. Estimate only as a last resort.

Print your own work-experience data in your *DataTrakt*. Start with your most recent job and work backward. Practice being neat.

Complete one work-experience form in your *DataTrakt* for each work experience you've had, regardless of how long you worked at the job or the type of work you did. There are separate work-experience forms in your *DataTrakt* for paid, unpaid (volunteer), and military experiences. If you worked as a volunteer, treat that experience just as if it were a paid position. Do the same with your military experience if you have been in the military.

IMPORTANT

If you need more forms for any of these three types of work experience, make copies before you use the last one.

The following tips will help you complete your *DataTrakt*. Remember to start with your most recent job and work backward through your work experience. When you finish, you should have a well-developed, positive outline of your work. This in itself will put you ahead of the average job-seeker. You will also find this information useful in many phases of your job-search.

Limited Work History

If you have little or no experience, make your education part of your work history. Evaluate your education just as if it were a job. This process is not easy, but it's worth it. It works especially well if you are or have been a vocational student. Review your list of transferable skills and self-management skills on pages 23, 24, and 27 for ideas. Evaluate the work you did as a homemaker just as if it were a business or a paying job. Most homemakers plan, budget, organize, supervise, and instruct — all of which are skills desired by employers.

Job Gaps

A **job gap** is a period of unemployment between jobs. If you had job gaps, you have to show the employer that you used your time for something constructive. Employers have the right to be suspicious of people who remain unemployed for over three months.

When no reason is given for a job gap, employers can only guess why the job-seeker was unemployed for so long. They might think that the gap resulted from the job-seeker's being judged unworthy by other employers. Any unexplained job gap will suggest, at the very least, that the applicant's qualifications are less than those expected by the employer.

If you do have a job gap of three or more months, there are several ways to handle it. Which way you use depends on what you did during that time.

Use the **good excuse** method when you did something that employers might find acceptable. This includes most worthwhile activities that cannot be done while working full time. You may have done such things as baby-sitting, yard work, or house painting, which can be called *self-employed*. If you took a trip, it could be listed as *travel*. If you obtained any type of schooling, list it as *education*. Whatever the good excuse, include it in the *DataTrakt*.

It is much better to have a **positive** explanation for your job gap than no explanation at all. Therefore, think carefully about what you did during that time. If you are not sure whether or not the reason sounds positive, ask for opinions.

If you have a job gap and no positive explanation, **do not** falsify your employment dates. You could lose your new job as a result. Instead, use a slightly different method to list the material. You can then explain this in an interview, if necessary. For example, Erin Martin has the following job history:

JOB 3 — Employed From *3-80* To *4-82*

JOB 4 — Employed From *12-78* To *11-79*

Notice that between the end of Job 4 (11-79) and the beginning of Job 3 (3-80), there is a gap of four months. To avoid showing a four-month job gap, she should use one of the example methods shown below. These methods are called *stretching*.

Example #1
   JOB 3 — *Employed from spring 1980 to spring 1982*
   JOB 4 — *Employed from winter 1978 to winter 1979*
Example #2
   JOB 3 — *Employed from 1980 to 1982*
   JOB 4 — *Employed from 1978 to 1979*

The **blank method** (omitting dates) can also be used to make job gaps less obvious. This method works best for job gaps of six months or longer. If you use the blank method on an application, be prepared to discuss the subject in an interview.

The following is an example of the blank method. All other data for Job 4 should be listed.

JOB 3 — Employed From *3-71* To *4-74*   **JOB 4** — Employed From _____ To _____

Reasons for Leaving

In the reasons-for-leaving part of your work experience, pay attention to how you word your responses. Do not write negative comments. Negative information on an application or in an interview may cause employers to doubt your value as an employee — even if your other qualities are outstanding. **Never** state your reason for leaving a position with **negative** phrases such as the following:

"I quit."   *"I had problems with co-workers."*

"I was fired."   *"The work was too hard."*

"I was terminated."   *"The pay was too low."*

"The job was too dirty."   *"I was arrested."*

"I had problems with the boss."

Whatever your reason for leaving a job, you should list only **positive** responses in your *DataTrakt*. The following examples may help you state your reason for leaving each position.

Reasons for Leaving

"I desired a more challenging position."

"I wanted a position with responsibility."

"I wanted work that was career-oriented."

"There was a general layoff in the plant."

"The work was seasonal (part time)."

"I became a full-time student."

"I began a long-planned tour of the U.S."

"I began self-employment."

"I had an option for a better job."

"I wanted to be more productive."

"I wanted a job requiring my best skills."

"I preferred a better work environment."

"I made a long-planned move to this area."

"I wanted a job in which I could learn."

"I desire a career-oriented position in (field in which you are applying)."

Check the flow of your *DataTrakt's reasons for leaving*. Start at the end of your list. Does the reason for leaving Job 4 support your having taken Job 3? Does the reason for leaving Job 3 support your having taken Job 2? Continue this questioning. Finally, the reason you left your last job should support your present job-search. Be sure everything implies a **positive** message.

Supervisor

List the name and title of the supervisor who knows your work best and will give you a good recommendation. If that supervisor is no longer with the company, use the name of someone who knows your work and is willing to act as your work reference. Obtain a letter of recommendation if possible since many organizations will not take references over the phone.

Days Missed

Your reliability will be judged by the number of days you've missed. If you have over six days of missed time per year, review the section on days missed in Chapter 3.

Supervisory Duties

Employers think that workers who can oversee the work of others are valuable employees. If you have supervised anyone, either formally or informally, enter the number of people you supervised and the duties these workers performed.

Data, People, Things, and Ideas

As you learned in Chapter 1, you can divide all work into four simple parts: **data, people, things,** and **ideas.** You will use these categories to collect and organize your work-experience information. Notice in your *DataTrakt* that there is a boxed area for each of these four categories. For each category you are to list your experiences.

- In the **data** section, list the ways in which you have used information, such as keeping time-card records, scheduling appointments, and keeping customer files.

- In the **people** section, list the people-oriented duties you've had, such as taking customer orders, working as a member of a team or group, and training new workers.

- In the **things** section, list the different kinds of work you've done with equipment, such as computers, nail guns, and ohm meters.

- In the **ideas** section, list the creative ideas you've had that have helped your company, such as devising a more efficient filing system or suggesting an improvement in a product or service.

For each category, list every possible experience you have had. Then, after completing each list, place a check in the column labeled *NJ* (Next Job) next to each item that you think will be related to your next job. You will want to focus on these things when you prepare for interviews. Also check either the *L* or *D* column to indicate that you *Liked* or *Disliked* that experience over 50 percent of the time.

Other Duties and Responsibilities

Reliable workers do more than the job description demands. Show the employer your reliability by identifying any duties not already listed. A responsibility is a *special* duty, such as opening and closing the store, purchasing materials, and training workers. Employers give these responsibilities only to the most reliable and skilled workers. List any situations in which you have had more responsibility than your co-workers. Then check the appropriate *NJ, L,* and *D* columns.

Work-Experience Statement

Employers generally expect you to describe your experience on applications and during interviews. Read the following examples of effective work-experience statements.

> *"I worked at Huron Metalworks for three years as a welder. I am skilled in precision fabrication and am able to both torch and arc weld. I'm sure I will be an excellent welder for you."*

> *"During the past four years I have been the Assistant Recreations Director at Sunrise Manor Retirement Village. This experience has given me practical insight into the needs and concerns of the elderly. I know that I communicate well with retirement-age people. I will be a dependable member of your Senior Citizens' Hotline staff."*

> *"I've worked at McCall's Family Restaurant for the past three years. I began as a dishwasher. I quickly progressed to busboy, then parking attendant. Later I was made responsible for the salad bar. I also filled in at the cash register. During the past two years I have been in charge of inventory, ordering, and banquet management. As the assistant manager of your cafe, I believe my varied experience will be most valuable."*

Now make a work-experience statement of your own. Choose the job listed in your *DataTrakt* that best shows your skills related to the job you want. Your statement should contain at least three sentences. The first should include your former employer's name. It should also include the length of time on the job and your titles. The second sentence should mention some skills gained from the former job that are related to the job you want now. The third sentence should explain the connection between this past experience and the job you are seeking. The examples above will help you if you're not sure what to write.

My Work-Experience Statement

_____

_____

_____

_____

_____

_____

_____

_____

Education and Training

Formal education and training is more important in some jobs than others. An employer may expect you to have a certain kind of education and training. This could include grammar school, high school, and college. It could also include technical school, business college, and military training.

Make sure that your education and training are completely described in your *DataTrakt*. The sample chart below and the following instructions will guide you as you fill in the Education and Training Section of your *DataTrakt*.

Sample Education and Training Chart

School	Name of School and Complete Address	From mo.	From yr.	From mo.	From yr.	Full Time	Part Time	Fields of Study and Special Courses	Number of Hours Completed	Diploma or Degree	Grade Point Average
Primary	ROACHDALE ELEMENTARY P.O. BOX 100 ROACHDALE, IN. 46172	9	56	5	62	✓	—	GENERAL		DIPLOMA	3.5 (4 pt. SCALE)
Junior High	FILLMORE JR. HIGH 100 S. MAIN ST. FILLMORE, IN. 46128	9	62	5	64	✓	—	GENERAL		DIPLOMA	3.6 (4 pt. SCALE)
Senior High	SOUTH PUTNAM COMMUNITY GREENCASTLE, IN. 46135	9	64	5	68	✓	—	major: COLLEGE PREP. minor: ART		DIPLOMA	3.2 (4 pt. SCALE)
College	OLIVET NAZARENE P.O. BOX 666 KANKAKEE, IL. 60901	9	67	1	70	✓	—	major: minor: ART	50 SEMESTER HOURS	—	3.2 (4 pt. SCALE)
Other	INDIANA STATE UNIVERSITY TERRE HAUTE, IND. 47809	6	74	5	76	✓	—	major: BROADCASTING minor: —	—	B.S. BROADCASTING	3.96 (4 pt. SCALE)
Other	20/20 OPTICS, INC. 1800 N. 7th ST. LINCOLN, NB. 68504	1	79	10	80	✓	—	major: APPRENTICE OPTICIAN minor:	—	CERTIFICATE OF COMPLETION	—
GED	Date Received:							Location			
Circle the highest grade completed:	1 2 3 4 5 6 7 8 9 10 11 12 13 14 15 (16) 16+										

Type of School

The column headed *school* lists the schools you are likely to have attended. Note the lower boxes marked *other*. In these spaces you should list any technical, business, or correspondence schools in which you enrolled. You should also list any programs in which you took part.

School Name and Address

In the second column, print the name, street address, city, state, and zip code of each school you attended.

From and To

State the number for the months and years that you started and finished at each school.

Full-time and Part-time

Place a check in the column (full-time or part-time) that best describes your schedule at each school.

Fields of Study and Special Courses

Under *Fields of Study and Special Courses*, write *general* for primary and junior high schools. Your high school studies may have been general, business, trades, or college prep. For colleges and other schools, state your major (and minor, if it applies).

Number of Hours Completed

Include the number of hours completed only if you did **not** receive a diploma or degree. Give the number of hours (months, years, semesters, semester hours, or quarter hours) completed when you left that school.

Diploma or Degree

If you graduated from primary and junior high schools, write *diploma* in the correct spaces. Do the same if you graduated from high school. If you graduated from college, include the type of degree and field of study. An example would be *B.S., Sociology*. Name any degree, diploma, certificate, license, or award received for completing other schools and training.

Grade Point Average

Your grade point average is your average grade for all the courses you took in a certain school. Always include the scale for evaluating the average (for example, 3.0 on a 4-point scale).

GED

If you have a General Education Diploma (GED), print the date you received it. Then print the name and address of the institution where you earned your GED.

Highest Grade Completed

At the bottom, indicate the number of the **last full year** of school successfully completed. For example, if you left high school during your senior year, circle *11*, the last **full** year completed.

Your Education and Training Statement

Now that you have compiled your education and training data, you can develop a statement you can use in interviews. You should be prepared to explain how your education and training relate to the position you want. The following explanation is an example:

"I took a first-aid course in high school. This course got me interested in nursing. I took a job as a nurse's aide after graduating. I was trained to take vital signs and do patient care. When I decided to become a practical nurse, I worked and trained at Regency. Now I have my degree. I think my training can be useful in this clinic."

```
┌─────────────────────────────────────────────────────┐
│             My Education and Training Statement       │
│                                                       │
│   _____ │
│                                                       │
│   _____ │
│                                                       │
│   _____ │
│                                                       │
│   _____ │
│                                                       │
│   _____ │
│                                                       │
│   _____ │
│                                                       │
│   _____ │
│                                                       │
│   _____ │
└─────────────────────────────────────────────────────┘
```

Job-Related Personal Information

Employers want to know everything about you that relates to their job opening. On the *DataTrakt* page titled *Job-Related Personal Information*, you will record a wide range of relevant data. You will use this data throughout your job-search.

Position Desired

As stated earlier, you should know what job you want and can do well before you write your *position desired*. This bit of data will provide the direction for your job-search. When you know what you want to do, print the title of that job in your *DataTrakt*.

Sometimes your first choice won't be available. Is there a second job for which you feel qualified and are willing to accept? If so, list this job as your **second choice**.

Salary Desired

If you know what salary you want, and it is a reasonable sum, record your desired salary. Otherwise, leave the space blank for now. You will read more about this subject in Chapter 3. That information may affect your decision about desired salary.

Availability

Think about when you will be available to start work. (Do not start a new job one week if you plan to take a trip or vacation the next week.) Decide what hours and days you will be available for regular work. Consider your life-style, family, and ability to adjust to a new schedule. Are you *really* willing to work weekends, overtime, and holidays? Lots of people say this until the time comes to show up for work. Don't say you are willing if you're really not. The best approach is to be as flexible as possible. You can always refuse a job offer later. Print in your *DataTrakt* the date, hours, and days that you will be available. Also indicate your willingness or unwillingness to relocate.

Certification, Registration, and Licenses

Information about certification, registration, and licenses is required on some applications. This is to determine whether or not you are qualified to practice a certain occupation. Electricians, medical technicians, nurses, and teachers are examples of workers who are certified. If you have professional certification, registration, or licenses, print the information in your *DataTrakt*. If not, put a dash in the space.

Some applications require your driver's license number. Some also ask what type of driver's license you have (such as operator or chauffeur). Print in your *DataTrakt* the information about your driver's license.

Professional Organizations

Professional organizations are established to promote the interests of certain vocational fields. Professional organizations may be either local, state, national, or international. Examples include state teachers' associations, the American Federation of Service Managers, the National Association of Computer Programmers, and the National Association of Broadcasters — to name a few.

In your *DataTrakt*, print the names of any professional organizations to which you belong. Also print other relevant data, such as your title (if you have one) or membership number. Put a short dash in each space if you do not belong to an organization.

Hobbies, Interests, and Leisure Activities

An interest is a personal feeling, concern, or curiosity about something. A hobby is similar to an interest; it is something you like to do or study in your spare time.

You may have interests or hobbies related to the job you are seeking. If so, an employer will realize that you will tend to like your work. Thus, you will probably perform better and stay on the job longer than other applicants. This helps make you the right person for the job.

If you have taken the time to find out what job you really want, you probably have interests and hobbies related to this type of work. If so, list these interests and hobbies in your *DataTrakt*.

Now read the following examples of interest and hobby statements made by other job-seekers.

"When I was in school I took all the bookkeeping, accounting, and math courses I could. Numbers fascinate me. I know I would enjoy being a bookkeeper with this firm."

"I want to be a dressmaker. My favorite hobby is making clothes for myself and my family. I would love to be a full-time seamstress."

"I've been interested in music all my life. I started piano lessons when I was six. Later I learned brass, percussion, and guitar. I compose and arrange my own songs. I have taught piano and guitar privately for four years. I would be a dedicated salesperson in your music store because I believe people should make their own music."

"I love flowers. My house is nearly a jungle of vines, buds, and bouquets. In the summer I have a large flower garden. I've taken courses in horticulture and floral arrangement from the free university. I'd truly enjoy working in your shop and greenhouse."

You should be prepared to make a statement similar to those in an interview. In the space below, write two simple statements about your interests and hobbies. Also show how that interest or hobby connects to your job objective and supports your entry into a particular line of work. These statements might help convince an employer that you are the right person for the job.

Interests and Hobbies

Statement: _____

_____

_____

Connection: _____

_____

_____

Interests and Hobbies

Statement: _____

_____

_____

Connection: _____

_____

_____

Successes and Achievements

For some strange reason, most people forget to discuss their personal, work, and social successes during the interview. Some people say, *"I don't want to toot my own horn," "sounds too much like bragging,"* or *"they should like me for what I am."* The Work Book response to these people is simple: *"How will employers get this important information about you unless you tell them?"*

Bobby Knight, the head basketball coach of Indiana University, says, *"If it's in the record book . . . it isn't bragging, it's fact."* Telling the facts about your successes is good strategy. You wouldn't want another applicant to talk about his or her successes and beat you out of the job, would you?

"What's a success?" you ask. It could be that you taught yourself to be a mechanic, that you have always done everything to perfection, or that you starred in a local theatrical production. Anything that you feel is a success is a success. In your *DataTrakt* list your life, work, and educational successes.

Now, from the successes listed in your *DataTrakt*, pick two or more that might show employers that you are better qualified than other applicants. Then write a statement that connects that success to the employer's expectations.

```
┌──────────────────────────────────────────────────────────────────────┐
│                     Successes and Achievements                         │
│                                                                        │
│   Statement: _____       │
│                                                                        │
│   _____         │
│                                                                        │
│   Connection: _____       │
│                                                                        │
│   _____         │
└──────────────────────────────────────────────────────────────────────┘


┌──────────────────────────────────────────────────────────────────────┐
│                     Successes and Achievements                         │
│                                                                        │
│   Statement: _____       │
│                                                                        │
│   _____         │
│                                                                        │
│   Connection: _____       │
│                                                                        │
│   _____         │
└──────────────────────────────────────────────────────────────────────┘
```

If you're on a "success roll," use a separate sheet of paper to identify and connect more of your successes.

Transferable Skills and Self-Management Skills

Your final exercise in this section is to review your lists of transferable skills and self-management skills on pages 23, 24, and 27 in Chapter 1.

Take what you consider to be your **top ten** entries from each and compare them with the type of work you are seeking. If you believe they match up well with the types of skills needed to do the job, list them in the transferable skills and self-management skills sections of you *DataTrakt* booklet. If your skills don't match up, go back through each list to identify your other skills that do match.

References

A reference is a person who will speak about your good qualities to an employer. The people you choose as references should know something about your work skills, personality traits, education, life experiences, and transferable skills. If you want your references to reinforce your employment value, they need to know about you and be willing to give a positive recommendation.

You might be thinking, *"Employers don't check references, do they?"* You bet they do if they're planning to stay in business. Choosing your references and keeping track of information about them is an important part of your job-search.

You want every reference to be **positive.** Choose your references with care. They should be people who can be contacted easily.

Later you will learn to make a *JIST Card* (Chapter 4). You also have the option of making a resume. You should give one of these tools to each of your references. In this way these people will be prepared to respond favorably in your behalf.

There are two types of references you will need to create: *personal references* and *employer references*. The following information will help you select your references and complete the reference forms in your *DataTrakt*.

Personal References

Select four people who know your work or character and will give you a good reference (instructors, good friends, neighbors, co-workers, and ministers, for example). Contact them to ask if they will agree to be your reference and if they are willing to respond to both phone and written inquiries.

Make sure they know the type of work you are seeking. Mention briefly what you would like them to say about you. Make sure they are comfortable with your summation of your skills. Never ask a reference to "bend the truth."

Send each reference some supportive materials, such as your resume and JIST Card, which they can use when asked to speak in your behalf. Whatever you supply, make sure it includes your job objective.

Fill out the Personal Reference form in your *DataTrakt* while you are talking with your references. Make sure you have all of the necessary information and that you have spelled their names correctly.

Employer References

A common problem question during interviews is *"What will your former employers say about you and your work?"* It is foolish to assume or hope that the information your past employers give will be in your best interest. Even a helpful employer can create a negative impression by not responding to a reference inquiry in a certain fashion. The Employer Reference Checklist forms in your *DataTrakt* will assist you as you contact former employers to ask very specific questions about your past work and performance.

Words of Caution

If there has been friction between you and a former employer, it is **your** responsibility to discuss the problem with that employer to try to improve the situation. Training materials can't do this for you. Discuss any problems you can't resolve with your job-search instructor.

For each paid, volunteer, and military Work Experience Evaluation form you complete, contact the employer and complete an Employer Reference Checklist on pages 18 and 19 of your *DataTrakt*. Although you may contact employers by phone or in person, face-to-face contact is best.

Tell the employer the type of work you are looking for. Mention that you are investing a lot of time and energy in preparing for your job-search and that you would appreciate five minutes of help. Read the information from the appropriate Work Experience Evaluation form and ask for **honest** comments, agreements, or disagreements. Record any negatives in the margins. Next, ask the employer to honestly evaluate each topic listed on your Employer Reference Checklist. Discuss problem areas and ask for help in correcting these.

You may also want to ask for letters of reference from former employers. If so, volunteer to write the letters yourself for the employers to sign.

USING YOUR *DATATRAKT*

Your *DataTrakt* should now contain most of the basic information that employers will want to know about you. Congratulations! You have just made a significant tool for your job-search. Due to the convenient size of your *DataTrakt*, you have a pocket or purse full of personal data.

Carry your *DataTrakt* with you throughout your job-search. Do not rely on memory, which can fail you. Your *DataTrakt* has all of the dates, telephone numbers, names, and addresses that few people could keep in their memory. It will give you the information and the confidence you need to meet the employers' expectations of appearance, dependability, and skills.

3 APPLICATIONS

... powering up

The *application* is the tool most familiar to job-seekers. It contains questions about a job-seeker's personal and work-related data. It is an employer's first introduction to a job-seeker. For most employers it is also a *screening device*, a way to eliminate undesirable applicants from consideration. Only if the application makes a good first impression will it lead to an interview.

Employers usually refer to applications during interviews. The application becomes the basis for most of the interview questions. The application also allows employers to compare the applicants. When a person is hired, the application becomes part of the employee's record.

In this chapter you will learn how to produce a near-perfect application and how to **power up** your application so that it screens you in, not out, of the running for the interview. This is especially important since only 1 percent of the applications completed actually lead to an interview!

After studying this chapter you should be able to make each application create a good first impression. This will insure your confidence and success in other areas, especially interviews. After you complete this chapter, your applications will meet the major employer expectations, which are

1. **Appearance** — Make your applications neat, complete, and accurate. Read and follow the application instructions as you transfer your *DataTrakt* information. In this way you will avoid making mistakes.

2. **Dependability** — You may be able to show your dedication to good attendance directly since many applications ask about attendance. You will show that you are dependable when you list previous responsibilities. You will soon discover that there are many other ways to express your dependability on an application.

3. **Skills** — You will list many of your skills directly on the application. The typical application is designed primarily for outlining the job-seeker's skills.

APPROACHING YOUR APPLICATION

During your job-search you will probably fill out many applications. To help insure that yours will be among the best that each employer sees, read and work carefully through the exercises that follow. Remember — the way you present your information is as important as its content.

Being Prepared

Be prepared to fill out an application whenever you apply for a job. To be prepared you need the following:

- **Erasable black, fine-tip pen** — to fill out the application
- **Your completed *DataTrakt*** — to provide you with all the information you will need
- **JIST Cards** (see Chapter 4) — to leave with the employer
- **6-inch ruler** — to help you write neatly
- **Small note pad** — to keep notes about applications and interviews
- **White out** (available at office supply stores) — to correct mistakes and remove smudges
- **Pencil and eraser** — to complete exercises and take tests
- **Small dictionary** — to check your spelling
- **Resumes** — to leave with the employer.

Following Instructions

Be sure to read the instructions before writing any data on an application. Many applications begin with general instructions, such as *Print in ink*, or *To be handprinted in ink*, or *typewritten*. Separate instructions may tell you how to present information for each section or item. Other instructions may tell you not to put any data in a certain space.

Following instructions is important. Employers want to hire people who can follow instructions on the job. Employers will not have a high regard for your dependability and skill if you cannot follow instructions on an application.

The Dash

Some application questions will not apply to you. Make a short dash (—) after each of these questions. The dash is a simple, attractive way to tell employers that you have read the question, but that it does not apply to you.

Blank Spaces

It is sometimes better to leave a blank space on your application than to write information that could hurt your chances of getting a job. An application will not get you a job. It can, however, keep you from being considered for a job. If an honest answer to an application question is negative or easily misunderstood, leave that item blank. Do not even make a dash in this space. You can explain the blank in the interview if necessary. In this way the blank will not automatically be used to screen you from a job for which you might otherwise qualify.

Expect employers to question you about blank spaces. Be prepared to answer their questions. If a blank space is not mentioned in the interview, be sure to mention it after you are offered the job. This will prevent you from being fired later for withholding information.

An alternative to leaving a space blank is to write *"Will explain in interview."* Decide for yourself which way is better for you.

The Sections

The bulk of this chapter deals with the sections common to most job applications. These sections fall into seven basic areas of information. The seven areas and the application sections that apply to each area are listed below.

1. **Identification**
   Name
   Social Security Number
   Address
   Telephone Number
   Physical Traits
   Date and Place of Birth
   Proof of Age
   Citizenship
   Emergency Information

2. **Family Relationships**
   Marital Status
   Dependents
   Family Names and Occupations

3. **Health**
   General Health
   Disabilities and Physical
      Limitations
   Emotional and Mental Disorders
   Family Illness
   Workers' Compensation
   Attendance

4. **Education**
   Education and Formal Training
   Future Schooling

5. **Position Desired**
   Position Desired
   Salary Desired
   Availability
   Transportation

6. **Experience**
   Work Experience
   Military Experience
   Volunteer Activities
   Certification, Registration, and
      Licenses
   Professional Organizations
   Clubs and Organizations
   Hobbies, Interests, and Leisure-
      time Activities
   Other Skills

7. **Miscellaneous**
   Future Plans
   References
   Arrest, Jail, and Conviction

Powering Up Your Application

You want to make sure that your application is one that will lead to an interview. Consider the "rules of thumb" listed below as you work your way through this chapter. These rules will help you produce the most persuasive, powerful application possible.

● **Realize that applications are "closed systems."** There's only so much space in each section and only so much room on each application to show employers how you will meet their expectations. This means that you must make every word count. To insure that you are using your space wisely, compare your information with the employer's expectations. If your information meets any one of the expectations, it's probably a good use of space.

- **Follow the rules . . . until they stop you from showing employers your value.** Most applications gather only basic information, and they don't do that very well. If you need to expand on information, develop a counter to a problem area, or if you just need more space, attach an extra sheet of paper or an index card. It's even okay to write in the margins and above or below words, **if you do it neatly.**

- **Do not use "lazy" responses.** Many people try to escape the work of completing the application by writing *"See attached resume."* Others, not wanting to write out the same information twice, simply state *"Same,"* or *"See above."* Neither of these tactics contributes to a persuasive, powerful application.

- **Counterbalance negative situations with positive information. Never** write negative information. If you choose to enter information that might be seen as negative (disabilities, reasons for leaving last job, etc.), you must also show the employer that you are able and willing to do everything necessary to get the job and do it well. You always have at least five options to problem sections. These options are
    1. Lie and try to get away with it. This is **not** advisable and is unfair to the employer.
    2. Use a dash (—) for problem sections, then discuss the topic during the interview.
    3. Tell the truth and present a counterbalancing statement on the form.
    4. Print *Will discuss in interview*. This may or may not help you.
    5. Leave the section blank and discuss it during the interview.

  Each situation is different, and only you can decide which of the options listed above is the right one for you in a particular situation. If you are not sure about what to do, discuss the options with your teacher or counselor.

- **Read the application front and back before completing.** Many application forms have a section on the last page that begins with the statement, "Do not write below this line." The information in this section often tells you how the employer will evaluate the applications. This can give you clues about how you should answer certain questions.

- **Re-do poorly done applications, if possible.** Many people wish they could go back and re-do the applications they completed poorly. Go to those places and tell the employer that you need to upgrade your information and would like a new application to complete. You want only good information in your file.

FILLING OUT AN APPLICATION

To learn how to fill out an application, follow the instructions for each exercise in this chapter. Listing your data correctly is as important as listing correct data.

For all the exercises, use a pencil so that you can make corrections. Neatly **print** your data. It is especially important that you use your *DataTrakt*. Your *DataTrakt* **must** be complete before you continue! If you are having trouble with your *DataTrakt*, consult a friend, relative, or vocational counselor for help. The *DataTrakt* will help you do the following exercises correctly and easily.

If you have a pencil and your completed *DataTrakt*, push onward.

Name

You may need to give your name many times on a basic application. The way you are asked to list your name may be different each time. Be sure to read the instructions before listing even this most familiar data. Generally your name will be one of the first bits of data required. You may be instructed to list your name on a vertical line along the edge of the application. This is for filing purposes.

You will need to sign most applications. Your signature is your name as you normally write it when signing checks and legal papers. You should carefully read and verify all statements on the application before signing it.

Never list a nickname on your job-search tools unless there is a special blank for it. You want to show employers that you are businesslike. Use your complete, legal name.

The following blanks are typical of the kinds you will find on applications. Print your name according to the instructions for each blank.

Print Name

_____
(Last)   (First)   (Middle Initial)

Name
_____
        First   Middle   Last

_____
(Applicant's Signature)

Print: Last Name, First Name, Middle Initial

Print Name

(Last)

(First)

(Middle)

Social Security Number

Be sure to print your social security number so that it is readable and correct. Many companies use their employees' social security numbers in filing and computer systems. An error in your social security number could cause problems with your payments, benefits, taxes, retirement, and unemployment account.

Your social security number should be printed correctly on your *DataTrakt*. Check your *DataTrakt* with your social security card right now. A little effort now can prevent big problems later. After all, you do not want *your* money to go into the wrong fund.

If you do not have a social security number, you should have already applied for one. If you have not yet applied, apply now at the nearest social security office or post office.

Social Security Number: _____

Address

All applications ask for your current address. Some also ask for your previous address. You may need to state how long you lived at each address. You already have this information in your *DataTrakt*. Rather than spending time remembering house numbers, zip codes, and dates, put your effort into transferring your data correctly to your application.

Before you list your address, read the instructions. Then be sure to put all your data in the correct spaces. If the application does not ask for a certain order, list, in the following order: street address; rural route, or box number; city; state; and zip code.

Address *1104 N. 4th St. Terre Haute, IN. 47807*

Consider how you will answer when asked how long you lived at a certain address. This information will give employers an impression of stability. Of course you want all impressions to be favorable. If you have lived at your current address for five years or more, you may choose to put a dash in the blank for previous address. If you have lived at your current address for a short time (less than two years), the length of time at your previous address may offset this. If both times are short, however, list only your current address. Then consider leaving the remaining address spaces blank. If you do this, be prepared to respond positively in an interview.

Following is an example of an address section commonly found on applications. Print your data in the correct spaces.

Address _____

How long have you lived at this address? _____

Previous Address _____

How long did you live at this address? _____

Telephone Number

Many employers prefer to contact applicants by telephone rather than by mail. This allows easy and immediate contact. It lets employers receive the applicants' responses right away.

Your telephone number could be as important in getting you employed as any other data on your application. Your phone should provide an open channel between you and an employer. Make sure you print your phone number correctly and neatly. The number should be the number of a phone that will be answered. If it is not, the channel to you is **not** open. The employer may contact the next-best applicant instead. To insure an open channel, follow the suggestions below before listing your phone number on an application.

Print the complete, correct number neatly. Begin with your area code. Then list the number. Do not guess! Many people have trouble remembering their own numbers since they seldom call home. Find your area code and phone number on the face of your telephone, in the phone book, or by calling directory assistance. (You should already have the number in your *DataTrakt*.) Note the following examples of complete, correctly written telephone numbers.

Telephone Number *(319) 555-0228* Telephone Number *(319) 555-0228*

Many businesses, schools, and large offices have switchboard-extension systems. If your phone is an extension unit, you will need to include your extension number. See the example below.

Telephone Number *(812) 555-0921, EXT. 21*

List a phone number that is likely to be answered during the day. If no one will be answering the phone, or if you do not have a phone, list the number of someone who can accept messages for you. This person should be a reliable friend or relative. Inform this person that potential employers might be calling. Choose someone who will be polite, take your messages accurately, and get word to you quickly.

It is a good idea to list **two** phone numbers. If the first number goes unanswered or is busy, employers can try your second number. Without a second number they might call the next applicant on their list. Therefore, list your home number and work number, or the number of a reliable friend. Most applications do not have separate blanks for two numbers. The examples below show how you may include two numbers.

Telephone Number *(611) 555-1116/555-7112*   Telephone Number *(611) 555-1116 (611) 555-7112*

Having a phone is a positive point for potential employees. If you have a phone, employers know they can contact you for overtime work or in an emergency. A telephone implies your stability within a community.

Print your complete, correct telephone number(s) in the space provided. If you have no number to write, put a dash above the line.

Telephone Number _____

Physical Traits

Applications may request a description of your physical traits. Some employers need this information for insurance or security reasons. Some jobs have certain height and weight restrictions (examples include the jobs of police officer and fire fighter). When listing your physical features on an application, print the correct and most current information. In the space below, print your basic physical traits.

Height _____   Hair Color _____

Weight _____   Eye Color _____

Note that you are not required to list race or color. There are a few exceptions, such as applications used to gather data about members of minority groups in government.

Date and Place of Birth

You must give your date of birth on some applications. It is important that you give the correct date. This date may be used to compute your insurance and retirement plans after you are hired. An application is no place for vanity with regard to your age. You can be fired for writing false information on an application. However, the law will be on your side if you are denied a job because of your age.

Application questions about age are stated in several ways. *Date of Birth, Birthdate, How Old Are You?* and *Age*, are a few examples. Dates are usually printed with numbers rather than words. For example, March 23, 1960 would be written as 3/23/60. Now print your data in the space provided below.

Birthdate _____ Date of Birth _____ Age_____
            (Day)   (Month)   (Year)   (Month) (Day) (Year)

Some applications ask for your place of birth. You need not include the name of the hospital or number of your delivery room. The city and state of your birth will do. Print the city and state where you were born.

Place of Birth _____

Proof of Age

If you are a young job-seeker, you may be asked to prove your age before an employer will consider hiring you. Most employers accept a driver's license as proof of age. If you do not have a driver's license, get a copy of your birth certificate or another legal document that shows your age. You can call or write the hospital where you were born for this information. The local Board of Health can also help you obtain a birth certificate.

If you are young, you may also need a work permit. You should phone your state's labor offices to find out if you need one.

Citizenship

Applications often include a question about citizenship. You must indicate whether or not you are a citizen of the United States. Noncitizens are usually asked to list their visa number and type. If you are not a U.S. citizen, but have applied for citizenship, give the date on which you applied. Note the following examples.

U.S. Citizen   ☑ Yes   ☐ No   U.S. Citizen   ☐ Yes   ☑ No
If no, list visa number and type: If no, list visa number and type: APPLIED
Number_____ Type_____   Number 317206D Type 7-12-82

In the space provided below, list your citizenship data.

U.S. Citizen   ☐ Yes   ☐ No
If no, visa number and type:

Number _____ Type _____

Emergency Information

Your application will be the start of your employee record after you are hired. Many applications will ask for the name and address of someone to contact in an emergency.

There are two reasons why you should answer these questions. The first reason is obvious — to be sure your family will be notified. The second reason is to show your stability. Employers might think you are a "drifter," and thus unreliable, if you do not list the name of someone who would be concerned about you.

You may list a close friend if no relatives live nearby. Otherwise, list a relative. Print your data in the form below.

In case of an emergency, contact:	
Name _____ Relationship _____	
Address _____	
Telephone Number _____ Business Number _____	

Marital Status

On all applications, list your marital status as either *married* or *single* — nothing else. Whatever your situation, it can be defined simply and honestly as either *married* or *single*. Other terms describing marital status may give employers a negative impression or invite them to pry into your personal life. Your interview will go smoothly if you avoid this potential trap.

Single best describes your status even if you are engaged, living with someone, or divorced. *Married* best describes your status even if you are separated.

The following two forms are common marital-status sections on applications. Indicate your data in the space provided.

Marital Status _____

Marital Status: (Check One)	☐ Married	☐ Single	☐ Engaged
	☐ Widowed	☐ Divorced	☐ Separated

If you listed anything other than *Married* or *Single*, read this section and do the exercise **again.**

Dependents

A *dependent* is anyone who relies on you as the major source of support. Most dependents are family members. Your spouse, children, and elderly parents are family members who could be dependents. When you are listing the number of your dependents, do not include yourself. If you have no dependents, put a dash in the space. Otherwise, print the number of dependents you have. Print your data at the top of the next page.

```
┌─────────────────────────────────────────────────────────────┐
│                                                               │
│   Number of Dependents_____│
│                                                               │
└─────────────────────────────────────────────────────────────┘
```

Some applications ask for the number of children you have and their ages. There are two questions employers may ask if you have young children. *"Will you have trouble finding a baby-sitter?"* *"Will you be taking a lot of time off work to care for your children?"* In our society women are still the main targets for these questions. If you have school-age children, you may choose to leave this section blank. If so, be prepared to discuss the matter if it comes up in the interview. Now print your own information.

```
┌─────────────────────────────────────────────────────────────┐
│                                                               │
│   Number of Dependents_____│
│                                                               │
│   Children _____ Ages _____│
│                                                               │
└─────────────────────────────────────────────────────────────┘
```

Family Names and Occupations

This section of information is rather dated. However, some applications still include it. It is best to be prepared. There may be questions about the names and occupations of your father, mother, and spouse. Employers may assume some things about you based on your family's background.

If you are asked for this data, list the present occupations of your family members. If a family member is retired or deceased, list that person's last occupation. If you are single, put dashes in the blanks for data about your spouse.

```
┌─────────────────────────────────────────────────────────────┐
│                                                               │
│   Father's Name  _____ Occupation _____│
│                                                               │
│   Mother's Name  _____ Occupation _____│
│                                                               │
│   Spouse's Name  _____ Occupation _____│
│                                                               │
└─────────────────────────────────────────────────────────────┘
```

General Health

Your health is quite important to your employer. The healthier you are, the more dependable you will be as an employee. Your employer will make more money if you are at work every day. You will make more money too. Therefore, it will benefit you the most if you can list your health as excellent.

Applicants often claim less-than-excellent health from habit. They sometimes list minor health problems. Everyone has small aches and pains from time to time. However, the application is not the place for complaints. Very few employers hire applicants due to sympathy.

When you answer questions about your health, first ask yourself, *"Will the way I feel keep me from doing the job I want?"* If the answer is *"no"* list your health as **excellent** — not good, but **excellent.**

If you have a health problem, discuss it with your doctor before job-hunting. Ask the doctor if the problem would in any way limit your work in your desired type of job. If your doctor thinks the problem would be limiting, ask for advice on how to handle this on applications. If your doctor advises you to avoid certain jobs, take that advice!

You may have a health problem that will **not** affect your ability to do the job you want. If so, do not note any negative information on your application. Leave the health sections blank if necessary. If you do this, be prepared to explain in an interview.

Read the following example. It is the kind of health form commonly found on applications. The applicant who filled out this form has had a history of heart trouble. However, the applicant knows what he wants to do and what he can do well. He is applying for a job that he could do well, even with his heart condition. Therefore, the applicant has listed his health as excellent.

In response to the *Have you ever had* section, the applicant left all the spaces blank. The employer might have noticed if all blanks but the *Heart-Trouble* blank had dashes. Note that the applicant has not checked *Back Pain, Headaches, Fainting or Dizzy Spells.* He has had these common aches and pains from time to time. However, these aches have nothing to do with the job he wants or his ability to perform it.

General Health: Poor ____ Fair ____ Good ____ Exellent ✓
Have you ever had: Tuberculosis _____ Heart Trouble _____
Epilepsy _____ Mental Illness _____ Back Pain _____
Headaches _____ Fainting or Dizzy Spells _____
Do you have any health limitations? _NO_
If Yes, explain _____
Do you have a chronic ailment or a congenital disorder? _____
If Yes, explain _____
Days of work/school missed in the last year? _NONE_
Physician _DR.J.L.Padgett_ Date last Physical _5/82_

Remember — the data you list on a job application should relate to that job. The applicant in the example had to answer the question, *"Do you have any health limitations that would affect your performance on the job?"* To this question, he answered *"no."*

Many applications ask about chronic ailments and congenital disorders. A *chronic ailment* is a physical problem that lasts a long time, or occurs again and again. A *congenital disorder* is a physical problem that has existed since birth. The applicant in our example has had his heart condition since birth. However, he did not list his chronic ailment and congenital disorder. Instead, he correctly chose to leave this question blank. Otherwise he might not get an interview. If asked, he will be ready to discuss his condition in the interview.

Many employers require physical exams for all new employees. If your exam shows that you have a serious health problem, an employer may decide not to hire you. However, this problem may not limit your ability to do a certain job. In this case, ask your own doctor to contact the employer's doctor. This may avoid many possible problems. If you have had a recent physical, be sure to say so. Mention that your health was found to be excellent and you are ready to start work immediately. How are you? Print the data about your health in the form below.

General Health: Poor_____ Fair_____ Good_____ Excellent_____

Have you ever had: Tuberculosis _____ Heart Trouble _____ Epilepsy _____

Mental Illness _____ Back Pain _____ Headaches _____ Dizzy Spells _____

Do you have any health limitations? _____

If Yes, explain _____

Do you have a chronic ailment or a congenital disorder? _____

If Yes, explain _____

Days of work/school missed in the last year _____

Physician _____ Date last Physical _____

Disabilities and Physical Limitations

The health sections of some applications ask about disabilities and physical limitations. If you have an *obvious* disability or limitation, deal with it directly in the interview, but not on the application. *Obvious* refers to the disabilities and limitations that employers can see. Also included are any problems noted by your personal physician and the company physician.

Applicants should not be discriminated against because of a disability. You should have taken your disability into account when choosing the job you wanted. Therefore, you already know that you **can do** this job. You will want to let the employer know this.

Do **not** list any disability or limitation (obvious or not) on an application. Leave the questions in this section blank. Deal with this subject **only** in the interview.

Do you have any physical disabilities or health limitations? _____

If Yes, explain _____

Emotional and Mental Disorders

Some health sections of applications ask whether or not you have, or have ever had, any emotional or mental disorders. Just as everyone has physical aches and pains from time to time, everyone gets the "blues" or feels nervous now and then. The "blues" is a form of depression. Nervousness is a form of anxiety. However, mild cases of depression or anxiety are not disorders.

Emotional and mental disorders have been misunderstood for a long time. Only since the beginning of this century have we begun to understand them. Today people can see counselors about their emotional and mental problems, just as they can see doctors about physical concerns.

You may have seen a counselor about an emotional or mental problem. If so, you should not be ashamed of the experience (just as there is no shame in seeing a doctor). However, it would not be wise to reveal this experience on an application. An employer who does not understand your situation might form a negative impression of you. If included, this kind of data might invite an interviewer to pry into your personal life.

Before you answer questions about your emotional and mental state, ask yourself, *"Will the way I feel keep me from doing the job I want?"* If your answer is *"no,"* put a dash in the appropriate blanks.

If you have been hospitalized or treated for an emotional or mental problem, you may have a gap in your job history. If so, you should have paid close attention to covering such gaps when you made your *DataTrakt*. Otherwise, the question remains, *"Will the way I feel keep me from doing the job I want?"* If you answer *"no,"* place a dash in blanks concerning emotional and mental disorder statements. The following is a sample question.

Have you ever been treated for an emotional or mental disorder? _____

If Yes, explain _____

Family Illness

Some applications ask about the health of family members. Unless you take care of an ill member of the family, put a dash in the blank provided. These questions do not relate to your desired job.

If you do care for a relative with a major illness, ask yourself, *"Will this keep me from doing my job well?"* If your answer is *"no,"* place a dash in the correct space. If you think your situation will often make you late for work or cause you to leave early, leave the space blank. Then be ready to discuss this in the interview. The following are two sample questions.

Do any members of your family have a major illness? _____ Mental illness? _____

Workers' Compensation

Do not confuse *workers' compensation* with *unemployment compensation*. This error could cost you a chance at an interview and a job. Be sure you know the difference between the two.

Workers' compensation is an employee benefit resulting from an injury on the job. Unemployment compensation (or unemployment *insurance*) is money paid to employees who have lost their jobs due to lay-offs or other factors beyond their control.

Many employers tend *not* to hire applicants who have received workers' compensation. These employers think (correctly or not) that someone who has drawn workers' compensation is unreliable. They think such workers are accident-prone and less able to do good work due to the injury. Employers may also think that such workers want to be paid for staying home.

If they do not apply to you, place a dash next to questions about workers' compensation. If they do apply to you, leave these questions blank. Then be ready to discuss this issue during an interview. Answer the following workers' compensation questions just as you will on an application.

Have you ever received workers' compensation? _____

If Yes, explain _____

Do you still have this problem? _____ Date of injury _____

Attendance

Attendance is part of the second major area of expectations — dependability. Other factors being equal, the best person for the job is the one who will be there every day. Most applications ask about your past attendance.

You may be asked, *"How many days of work or school did you miss last year?"* This question does not ask about vacation days or holidays. It refers to days missed when you were expected to attend. This includes any *sick days* taken, even if these days were allotted you by your employer. Of course, the fewer days missed, the more dependable you will seem to employers.

Print *none* if you did not miss any days of work last year. Perfect attendance deserves more emphasis than a dash can give. If you missed more than ten days of work, leave the space blank. As always, if you leave the space blank, be ready to discuss the subject in an interview.

> How many days of work or school did you miss last year? _____
>
> Explain _____

Education and Formal Training

All applications ask about your educational history. Most applications require quite a bit of information in this section. You will be able to give complete, accurate information by using your *DataTrakt*. The *DataTrakt* section on education and training is typical of similar sections on applications. Refer to the *DataTrakt* in the following discussion.

You should include the full names and addresses of the standard schools — primary through college. Spaces marked *Other* let you list technical schools, business colleges, correspondence schools, and on-the-job training. List military training and volunteer training in this section if they are not asked for elsewhere on the application.

You should be able to account for all the time you spent in school and training. This information could be important in explaining gaps in your job history. List the number of hours completed for any unfinished course of study or training. For instance, if you left high school after your third year, list the number of completed semester hours or semesters. This would help offset your lack of a diploma. Otherwise, you would leave this space blank and discuss it during an interview.

Notice that a space for listing a GED (General Education Diploma) is provided on the form. Be sure to list your GED if you have one. Some applications will not ask for this information specifically. In either case, print the data about your GED in either the blanks marked *High School* or *Other*. Here are two examples of how to include your GED data.

School	Name of School and Complete Address	From mo.	From yr.	To mo.	To yr.	Full Time	Part Time	Fields of Study and Special Courses	Number of Hours Completed	Diploma or Degree	Grade Point Average
Other	Johnson Education Center, 1100 N. 4th St. Carlin, CA. 95872	8	79	4	80	—	✓	GED	—	DIPLOMA	—

School	Name of School and Complete Address	From mo.	From yr.	To mo.	To yr.	Full Time	Part Time	Fields of Study and Special Courses	Number of Hours Completed	Diploma or Degree	Grade Point Average
GED	Johson Education Center, 1100 N. 4th St. Carlin, CA. 95872	8	79	4	80	—	✓	GENERAL	—	DIPLOMA	—

Some applications ask you to show the highest grade you completed. As with all your data, be accurate and neat. If you have a GED, refer to it here. Note the following examples.

What is the highest grade you have completed? ____*GED*_____

Circle the highest grade completed:	1	2	3	4	5	6	7	8	9	10	11	12 (GED)	13	14	15	16	16+

If you have not had much education or training, you may choose to skip the education section of an application. Knowing what you want to do and being able to do it well, is the important thing. If you have these qualities, you can convince an employer during the interview that you are the right person for the job.

Print your education and training data in the following form as you would on an application. This exercise will be easy if you consult your *DataTrakt*.

School	Name of School and Complete Address	From mo.	From yr.	To mo.	To yr.	Full Time	Part Time	Fields of Study and Special Courses	Number of Hours Completed	Diploma or Degree	Grade Point Average
Primary											
Junior High											
Senior High								major: minor:			
College								major: minor:			
Other								major: minor:			
Other								major: minor:			
GED	Date Received:							Location:			
Circle the highest grade completed:	1 2 3 4 5 6 7 8 9 10 11 12 13 14 15 16 16+										

Future Schooling

Applications often ask, *"Do you plan any future schooling?"* Answer in terms of classes or training that would benefit your work in the job you want. You may plan future schooling that is not work related. If you mention this, the employer may think your interests lie elsewhere. If you are not interested in work-related schooling, put a dash in the space provided for your answer.

Employers appreciate workers who want to learn more about job-related tasks. Some companies provide optional training. Others provide funding for books and courses. Some even pay for transportation, room, board, and tuition to educate their employees. Promotions and raises often depend on special training.

You may want to leave the future-schooling question blank if you are not sure of your plans. You can discuss this issue during an interview. Just remember that the job is your main interest.

If you **do** plan to get work-related training, indicate this on the application. Be prepared to answer interview questions about the classes or training you want. Tell the employers how your schooling will benefit their companies.

Do you plan any future schooling? *Yes, in work-related field.*

Give this some serious thought, then print *your* answer in the form at the top of the next page.

Do you plan any future school? _____

Titles

You should have already decided on the work you want to do. You had to make this decision to get the most value from this book. More important, you had to decide in order to succeed in your job-search and be happy with your work.

Most applications ask you to state the position desired. This helps employers evaluate all the other information given. If you list the position desired as "just any job" you cannot hope to make a good impression. The other information on the application will probably not indicate an ability to do *"just any job."* However, you will be appreciated by employers if you know which job you want.

Your main concern when stating your desired position is to keep open several options. You know what you want, so list the title of that job. Also include titles of similar or related positions. Note the following examples.

Position Desired *WAREHOUSE WORKER* Position Desired *WAREHOUSE WORKER*
        (SHIPPING CLERK, DRIVER)   *(OR SIMILAR POSITION)*

By showing employers that you have a specific goal, but are open to options, you increase your chances of being employed. Print the titles of your desired positions in each of the following sample forms.

Position Desired _____

Type of Work Desired: (check one)

Sales _____ Office _____ Warehouse _____ Mechanical _____

Electrical _____ Other (specify) _____

Salary Desired

Applications commonly provide space for you to specify your desired salary. This subject can pose a problem if you have not researched the job market. You do not want to undersell yourself. Nor do you want to price yourself out of the market with a wild guess. You can research the job market by following the suggestions below.

- Read want-ads that list salaries for similar positions.
- Call your local employment office and ask the salary range for your type of job.
- Talk with people who do the kind of work you want.

You may list a specific salary, a high-low range, or leave the space blank. However, the best response is to print *Open*. This is a positive word. It will not commit you to a figure either too low or too high.

Salary questions on an application (or in an interview) are based on one of five basic pay periods: hours, weeks, two-week periods, months, and years. You should determine your desired salary in terms of each pay period.

What salary do you desire? The following items are commonly found on applications. Print your answers for each after you have researched the subject.

Annual Salary _____ Monthly Salary _____ Two-Week Salary _____

Weekly Salary _____ Hourly Wage _____

Availability

Questions about when you will be available for work are often included on applications. This data will help employers make schedules that satisfy everyone.

You may be asked to state the date that you can start work. The day you give should fit your schedule. Do not start a job one week and expect to take a vacation the next. Do not begin a job one day if you intend to keep a dental appointment the next.

You may be asked to list the hours you will be available for work. The best response is *All Shifts*. This shows your flexibility. If your life-style, family, or other factors limit you to a certain shift, you can refuse job offers for other shifts. If an employer has already determined that you are the right person for the job, you might be changed to your desired shift.

You may be asked to list the days you will be available for work. The best response here is *All Days*. Many jobs consist of a Monday-to-Friday work week with possible overtime on weekends. Some jobs regularly include weekend work. On other jobs the work schedules change every week or month. The more flexible you are, the greater your chances of being interviewed and hired.

You should already have your availability data recorded in your *DataTrakt*. Refer to *Other Personal Information* in your *DataTrakt* and answer the following questions.

Availability: Date _____ Hours _____ Days _____

Transportation

Some application questions are concerned with transportation. They help employers determine whether you can be at work regularly and on time.

Your means of transportation should imply dependability. Your own car, a car pool, a public bus, and commuter trains are dependable forms of transportation. Calling a cab, depending on someone to drive you to work, and hitchhiking will **not** impress employers.

Print the data concerning your means of transportation in the spaces at the top of the next page.

```
┌────────────────────────────────────────────────────────────────────┐
│                                                                      │
│   Do you own a car? _____  Transportation _____    │
│                                                                      │
│   How will you get to work? _____        │
│                                                                      │
└────────────────────────────────────────────────────────────────────┘
```

If you will use public transportation to get to an interview (and the job), find out the number, route, schedule, and fare beforehand.

Some applications also ask for the number and type of your driver's license. This data is very important if you are applying for a job as a driver. In other jobs you may need to use company vehicles at certain times. This license information may be in your favor, so be prepared. Print your data below. Refer to your *DataTrakt*.

```
┌────────────────────────────────────────────────────────────────────┐
│                                                                      │
│   Driver's License Number _____  Type _____  Expiration _____ │
│                                                                      │
└────────────────────────────────────────────────────────────────────┘
```

Work Experience

On almost every job application *Work Experience* requires more data than any other section. Generally employers regard this as the most important part of an application. It should help you since it shows your skills.

You should be well prepared to list your work history. Your *DataTrakt* has all the work-experience data needed to fill out an application. Make sure your *DataTrakt* is complete. Use it when you list your work experience on an application.

Refer to your *DataTrakt* now. Use it to complete the following work-experience forms. List the data for your most recent job **first.** List your next most recent job in the next form, and so on. Notice that each form is different. Print your data according to the instructions for each form. If you have no work experience, leave the forms blank. You should be prepared to offset this during an interview.

EMPLOYMENT EXPERIENCE				
Dates Employed	Company Name and Address	Position Held	Salary	Reason for Leaving
FROM / / TO / /	COMPANY NAME / ADDRESS	1. / 2. / 3.	INITIAL $ PER / FINAL $ PER	

	EMPLOYER	DATES OF WORK	JOB TITLE & DUTIES	REASON FOR LEAVING
Name / Street / City & State		MONTH-YEAR From / To / Starting Salary / Leaving Salary	Supervisor	

WORK EXPERIENCE:						
DATES		NAME AND ADDRESS OF EMPLOYER	SUPERVISOR'S NAME AND TITLE	RATE OF PAY	DESCRIBE YOUR WORK	REASON FOR LEAVING
FROM	TO					

EMPLOYMENT RECORD		
EMPLOYER-NAME/ADDRESS	JOB TITLE	REF. CHK'D OFF. USE ONLY
	NAME OF SUPERVISOR	
	EMPLOYED FROM TO	SALARY
	NAME WORKED UNDER	
	REASON FOR LEAVING	

Military Experience

Most applications ask for data about military experience. The amount of information requested can range from a few lines to a detailed history.

If you were honorably discharged, you should accurately list all the data required. Consult your *DataTrakt*. If you received something less than an honorable discharge, leave this section blank. In this case, be prepared to discuss your military background in an interview. Be ready to give reasonable, positive answers. Put a dash in each blank if you were never in the service or never registered for the draft.

If you were honorably discharged, you are eligible for *Veterans' Preference Points*. These points help you get certain government jobs. Keep this in mind as you begin your job-search. To be credited with these points, you may need to obtain special forms. Ask you local Veterans' Administration Office for details. If you are a Vietnam veteran and are having trouble finding work, contact the V.A. Office. Many of these offices have job-placement programs and offer career counseling.

Volunteer Experience

List all of your volunteer experience on applications. Volunteer experience is a type of work experience and just as important. Volunteer activities usually require certain duties, responsibilities, and training. Information about these activities will meet two of the employer's main expectations — dependability and skill. This data may also cover a potential job gap.

Many applications have special sections for data about your volunteer experience. Others do not. If there is no special section, list your volunteer activities in the work-experience section.

Certification, Registration, and Licenses

Some applications provide space to list the professional and legal documents required for certain certifications. These documents are necessary in such fields as medicine, law, engineering, teaching, aviation, and accounting. If you have any professional certifications, registrations, or licenses, print your data in the form at the top of the next page. Consult your *DataTrakt*. Put a dash in each space that does not pertain to you.

Are you currently certified, registered, or licensed in any profession? _____

If Yes, give complete information, including number and expiration date, if any:

_____

Professional Organizations

Employers may be interested in the professional organizations to which you belong. Such a membership is especially important if the organization and job are directly related. However, membership in any professional organization supports your dependability and skill.

Include any titles when you list your professional organizations. Read the example form below. Then refer to your *DataTrakt*. Print your data in the blank form provided. Place a dash in the spaces if you do not belong to any professional organizations. (Do not list social organizations or activities.)

List the professional organizations to which you belong:

<u>NATIONAL ASSOCIATION OF BROADCASTERS</u>   <u>WIDGET MAKERS OF AMERICA, TREASURER</u>

List the professional organizations to which you belong:

_____   _____

Clubs and Organizations

Some applications ask about the clubs and nonprofessional organizations to which you belong. This information gives employers a more personal impression of you. Membership in a club or organization indicates an active person who can "get along" with other people. Being active and sociable are positive worker traits.

If you do not belong to any organizations and do not take part in activities outside of school or work, place a dash after such questions. It is also better to use a dash than to list membership with controversial organizations. Otherwise, list your clubs, organizations, activities, and titles if you have any. Read the following examples, then list your own data.

List clubs and organizations to which you belong <u>4-H CLUB, SECRETARY</u>

<u>JOGGING CLUB, MEMBER</u>

List any extracurricular activities <u>VOLUNTEER LEAGUE, JUNIOR VOLUNTEER.</u>

List clubs and organizations of which you are a member _____

_____

List any extracurricular activities _____

Hobbies, Interests, and Leisure-time Activities

An employer may have a special interest in you if one of your hobbies closely relates to your desired job. This can save the employer time and money since you will need less training than other job-seekers. You will also be more apt to stay with the job because it will be personally satisfying. Note the example below. The position desired by this applicant is electronics technician.

List your hobbies, interests and leisure-time activities.

As a "ham" radio operator, I enjoy designing and building my own equipment. I do extensive reading in technical journals concentrating on the development of new techniques, etc.

Determine which of your hobbies, interests, and leisure-time activities relate to your desired position. List those that most closely relate to this position. Print them in the first column of blanks below. Refer to your *DataTrakt*.

Hobbies   **Relation**

_____   _____

_____   _____

_____   _____

_____   _____

_____   _____

In the second column, explain how each hobby relates to the position you want. You will use only the data in the left-hand column on applications. You can use the information in the second column during an interview. Refer to Chapter 2 as you fill in the left-hand column.

Other Skills

Applications often ask for other skills, abilities, experience, and training related to your desired job. This section may reveal some of your best qualifications. Most of these qualifications have been recorded in your *DataTrakt*. However, there may be some that you have not yet included in your *DataTrakt*. You may have some special qualifications that do not quite fit any other category. You cannot list too many. Consult your *DataTrakt*. Also try to think of items you may have overlooked. Then print your data for the following typical question.

Other skills, abilities, experience, or training related to the position:

_____

_____

_____

Future Plans

Application questions about future plans are concerned with your motivation and dependability. This question is used frequently to screen out applicants who do not provide positive answers. Employers want to hire people who will stay with the company. It takes time and money to recruit, hire, and train new employees. Even with training, new employees need time to reach full productivity. Employees who do not stay on the job cost their employers time and money. The employers then must spend more time and money to find and train replacements. Thus, it is good business for employers to hire dependable people in the first place. This means that it is a good idea for you to show dependability. When answering questions about future plans, indicate one or more of the following plans.

- Progress within the company

- Improve productivity or quality

- A career with the company

- Learn more about the company and the job you want

You should be able to state an honest goal for your future in the job you really want to do and believe you can do well. Print your job-related plans in the space below.

What are your future plans? _____

_____

References

Most applications ask for a brief list of references. If you followed the directions in Chapter 2, you already have lists of both personal and employer references in your *DataTrakt*. You must make sure you have your *DataTrakt* with you when you fill out applications; otherwise it will be impossible for you to remember all of your reference information.

Arrest, Jail, and Conviction

Many applications ask if you have ever been arrested, jailed, or convicted for an offense other than a traffic violation. If these situations do not relate to you, place a dash in the space provided. If they do apply to you, there are things you should know before answering questions in this section.

Anything short of a felony conviction would be difficult for an employer to check. Typically, this kind of information is not made available unless you have signed a release form. If your situation did not result in a felony conviction, put a dash in each space provided.

If you have been convicted of a felony, leave these spaces blank. If you have served a sentence, you need not mention the subject. You should be prepared to discuss it briefly and positively in an interview. If you must discuss the subject in an interview, move on to your positive qualifications at the first opportunity.

Do not list a conviction on an application if you are on parole. Leave spaces blank for questions about arrests, jail, and convictions. However, you should be ready to discuss this in an interview. Your parole officer will probably contact your employer after you are hired. The following question is commonly found on applications. Record your data at the top of the next page.

Have you ever been arrested for other than a minor traffic violation? _____

If Yes, explain _____

Consider the following points if you have ever been convicted of a felony.

- Bonding is sometimes required before an employer can hire someone convicted of a felony. Ask your local employment office for help if you may need to be bonded.

- You would be wise not to seek a position related to your conviction. For instance, if you were convicted for selling drugs, do **not** apply for a nurse's aide position.

- You may have gaps in your job history due to spending time in jail. You should have attended to such gaps in the work-experience section of your *DataTrakt*.

USING YOUR APPLICATION

Applications are the only job-search tools used by the average job-seeker. The typical job-seeker goes to a company, asks for an application, tries to fill it out from memory, and then waits for the employer's call. An active (but still average) job-seeker will use this same approach, but much more often. This approach works, but it does not work very well. Since only one tool is used, success depends greatly on how well the tool has been made. In this situation the only other factor in determining success is luck.

Having completed this chapter, you will do better filling out applications than will other applicants. This means that you are likely to get more interviews than the average job-seeker. Your application will provide a positive view of who you are, relative to the job you want. Your application will meet each of the employer's major expectations. Its appearance will be neat (type if your printing is messy) and professional. It will show your dependability by listing your past responsibilities. And, it will show your skill by listing your education and experience.

Your application will be a strong tool. It is, however, **only one tool.** You need to learn about other tools you can use in your job-search. JIST Cards, telephone contacts, resumes, and the all-important interviews are tools explained in the next chapters. Use applications well. But do not be like the average job-seeker and limit yourself to applications alone.

Before learning about other job-search tools, make sure you have learned your lessons about applications well. The following exercise form resembles a typical application. During your job-search, you can expect to see applications requiring different degrees of detail. Some are simpler than this sample, some are more complex. Still, your work in this exercise will prepare you for most applications. Refer to your *DataTrakt* as you do the exercise. Use a pen with either black or blue ink. Take care to transfer your data neatly, without mistakes. **Print** your information unless instructed to do otherwise. Read and follow all instructions.

Remember — **Include only positive information on applications.** Turn back to the appropriate section of this chapter if you have questions about how to answer a particular item.

Ask a friend or counselor to review your work after you have finished. Have you followed all instructions? Have you been neat, complete, and accurate? Can you make any corrections or improvements?

Personal Qualifications Statement

Read instructions before completing form

1. Kind of position *(job)* you are filing for *(or title and number of announcement)*

2. Options for which you wish to be considered *(if listed in the announcment)*

3. Home phone
   Area Code | Number

4. Work phone
   Area Code | Number | Extension

5. Sex *(for statistics only)*
   ☐ Male ☐ Female

6. Other last names ever used.

Name *(Last, First, Middle)*

Street address or RFD no. *(include apartment no., if any)*

City | State | ZIP Code

8. Birthplace *(City & State, or foreign country)*

9. Birth date *(Month, day, year)*

10. Social Security Number

11. If you have ever been employed by the Federal Government as a civilian, give your highest grade, classification series, and job title.

Dates of service in highest grade *(Month, day, and year)*

From   To

12. If you currently have an application on file with the Office of Personnel Management for appointment to a Federal position, list, (a) the name of the area office maintaining your application, (b) the position for which you filed, and *(if appropriate)* (c) the date of your notice of rating, (d) your identification number, and (e) your rating.

13. Lowest pay or grade you will accept.
   PAY | GRADE
   $ per | OR

14. When will you be available for work? *(Month, and year)*

DO NOT WRITE IN THIS BLOCK
FOR USE OF EXAMINING OFFICE ONLY

Material
☐ Submitted
☐ Returned

Entered register

Notations:

Form reviewed:

Form approved:

Option	Grade	Earned Rating	Preference	Aug. Rating
			☐ 5-Points (Tent.)	
			☐ 10 Pts. 30% or More Comp. Dis.	
			☐ 10 Pts. Less Than 30% Comp. Dis.	
			☐ Other 10 Points	
Initials and date			☐ Disallowed	
			☐ Being Investigated	

THIS SPACE FOR USE OF APPOINTING OFFICER ONLY
Preference has been verified through proof that the separation was under honorable conditions, and other proof as required.

☐ 5-Point | ☐ 10-Points 30% or More Compensable Disability | ☐ 10 Points Less Than 30% Compensable Disability | ☐ 10-Point Other

Signature and title

Agency | Date

(right margin: ANNOUNCEMENT NO.   STATEMENT NO.)

---

15. Are you available for temporary employment lasting:

(Acceptance or refusal of temporary employment will not affect your consideration for other appointments.)

	YES	NO
A. Less than 1 month?		
B. 1 to 4 months?		
C. 5 to 12 months?		

16. Are you interested in being considered for employment by:

	YES	NO
A. State and local government agencies?		
B. Congressional and other public offices?		
C. Public international organizations?		

17. Where will you accept a job?

	YES	NO
A. In the Washington, D.C. Metropolitan area?		
B. Outside the 50 United States?		
C. Anyplace in the United States?		
D. Only in *(specify locality)*		

18. Indicate your availability for overnight travel:

A. Not available for overnight travel		
B. 1 to 5 nights per month		
C. 6 to 10 nights per month		
D. 11 or more nights per month		

19. Are you available for part-time positions *(fewer than 40 hours per week)* offering:

	YES	NO
A. 20 or fewer hours per week?		
B. 21 to 31 hours per week?		
C. 32 to 39 hours per week?		

20. Veteran Preference. Answer all parts. If a part does not apply to you, answer "NO".

	YES	NO
A. Have you ever served on active duty in the United States military service? *(Exclude tours of active duty for training in Reserves or National Guard)*.		
B. Have you ever been discharged from the armed services under other than honorable conditions? You may omit any such discharge changed to honorable or general by a Discharge Review Board or similar authority). If "YES", give details in item 34.		
C. Do you claim 5-point preference based on active duty in the armed forces? If "YES", you will be required to furnish records to support your claim at the time you are appointed.		
D. Do you claim 10-point preference? If "YES", check the type of preference claimed and complete and attach Standard Form 15, "Claim for 10-Point Veteran Preference," together with the proof requested in that form.		

Type of Preference: ☐ Compensable Disability 30% or More | ☐ Compensable Disability Below 30% | ☐ Non-compensable Disability | ☐ Purple Heart Recipient | ☐ Spouse | ☐ Widow(er) | ☐ Mother

E. List dates, branch, and serial number of all active service *(enter "N/A", if not applicable)*

From   To   Branch of Service   Serial or Service Number

(Continued on next page)

66

21. Experience. Begin with current or most recent job or volunteer experience and work back. Account for periods of unemployment exceeding three months and your residence address at that time on the last line of the experience blocks in order of occurrence.

May inquiry be made of your present employer regarding your character qualifications, and record of employment? *(A "NO" will not affect your consideration for employment opportunities except for Administrative Law Judge positions.)* ☐ YES ☐ NO

A

Name and address of employer's organization *(include ZIP Code, if known)*	Dates employed *(give months and year)* From To	Average number of hours per week
	Salary or earnings Beginning $ per Ending $ per	Place of employment City State

Exact title of your position	Name of immediate supervisor	Area Code Telephone number	Number and kind of employees you supervise
Kind of business or organization *(manufacturing, accounting, social services, etc)*	If Federal service, civilian or military, series, grade or rank, and date of last promotion.		Your reason for wanting to leave

Description of work *(Describe your specific duties, responsibilities and accomplishments in this job)*

For agency use *(skill codes, etc.)*

B

Name and address of employer's organization *(include ZIP code, if known)*	Dates employed *(give month and year)* From To	Average number of hours per week
	Salary or earnings Beginning $ per Ending $ per	Place of employment City State

Exact title of your position	Name of immediate supervisor	Area Code Telephone number	Number and kind of employees you supervised
Kind of business or organization *(manufacturing, accounting, social services, etc.)*	If Federal service, civilian or military series, grade or rank, and date of last promotion		Your reason for leaving

Description of work *(Describe your specific duties, responsibilities and accomplishments in this job)*

For agency use *(skill codes, etc.)*

C

Name and address of employer's organization *(include ZIP code, if known)*	Dates employed *(give month and year)* From To	Average number of hours per week
	Salary or earnings Beginning $ per Ending $ per	Place of employment City State

Exact title of your position	Name of immediate supervisor	Area Code Telephone number	Number and kind of employees you supervised
Kind of business or organization *(manufacturing, accounting, social services, etc.)*	If Federal service, civilian or military series, grade or rank, and date of last promotion		Your reason for leaving

Description of work *(Describe your specific duties, responsibilities and accomplishments in this job)*

For agency use *(skill codes, etc.)*

22. **A.** Special qualifications and skills *(skills with machines, patents or inventions, your most important publications [do not submit copies unless requested]; your public speaking and publications experience, membership in professional or scientific societies, etc.)*

B. Kind of license or certificate *(pilot, registered nurse, lawyer, radio operator, CPA, etc.)*	**C.** Latest license or certificate		**D.** Approximate number of words per minute	
	Year	State or other licensing authority	Typing	Shorthand

23. **A.** Did you graduate from high school or will you graduate within the next nine months, or do you have a GED high school equivalency certificate?

B. Name and location *(city and State)* of latest high school attended

Yes	Month and Year	No	Highest grade completed

C. Name and location *(city, State, and ZIP Code, if known)* of college or university. *(If you expect to graduate within nine months, give MONTH and YEAR you expect to receive your degree.)*

Name and location	Dates Attended		Years Completed		No. of Credits Completed		Type of Degree *(e.g., B.A.)*	Year of Degree
	From	To	Day	Night	Semester Hours	Quarter Hours		

D. Chief undergraduate college subjects	No. of Credits Completed		**E.** Chief graduate college subjects	No. of Credits Completed	
	Semester Hours	Quarter Hours		Semester Hours	Quarter Hours

F. Major field of study at highest level of college work

G. Other schools or training *(for example, trade, vocational, Armed Forces or business).* Give for each the name and location *(city, State and ZIP Code, if known)* of school, dates attended, subjects studied, number of classroom hours of instruction per week, certificate, and any other pertinent data.

24. Honors, awards, and fellowships received

25. Languages other than English. List the languages *(other than English)* in which you are proficient and indicate your level of proficiency by putting a check mark (✓) in the appropriate columns. **Candidates for positions requiring conversational ability in a language other than English may be given an interview conducted solely in that language.** Describe in item 34 how you gained your language skills and the amount of experience you have had *(e.g., completed 72 hours of classroom training, spoke language at home for 18 years, self-taught, etc.).*

Name of Language(s)	PROFICIENCY							
	Can Prepare and Deliver Lectures		Can Converse		Have Facility to Translate Articles, Technical Materials, etc.		Can Read Articles, Technical Materials, etc., for Own Use	
	Fluently	With Difficulty	Fluently	Passably	Into English	From English	Easily	With Difficulty

26. References: List three persons who are NOT related to you and who have definite knowledge of your qualifications and fitness for the position for which you are applying. Do not repeat names of supervisors listed under Item 21, Experience.

Full Name	Present Business or Home Address *(Number, Street, City, State and ZIP Code)*	Telephone Number *(Include Area Code)*	Business or Occupation

Answer Items 27 through 33 by placing an "X" in the proper column	YES	NO

27. Are you a citizen of the United States? ....
   If "NO", give country of which you are a citizen

NOTE: A conviction or a firing does not necessarily mean you cannot be appointed. The circumstances of the occurrence(s) and how long ago it (they) occurred are important. Give all the facts so that a decision can be made.

28. Within the last five years have you been fired from any job for any reason? ....

29. Within the last five years have you quit a job after being notified that you would be fired? ....
   If your answer to 28 or 29 is "YES" give details in Item 34. Show the name and address *(including ZIP Code)* of employer, approximate date, and reasons in each case. This information should agree with your answers in Item 21. Experience.

30. A. Have you **ever** been convicted, forfeited collateral, or are you now under charges for **any felony** or **any** firearms or explosives offense against the law? *(A felony is defined as any offense punishable by imprisonment for a term exceeding one year, but does not include any offense classified under the laws of a State as a misdemeanor which is punishable by a term of imprisonment of two years or less)* ....

   B. During the past seven years have you been convicted, imprisoned, on probation or parole or forfeited collateral, or are you now under charges for any offense against the law not included in A above? ....

NOTE: When answering A and B above, you may omit (1) traffic fines for which you paid a fine of $50.00 or less, (2) any offense committed before your 18th birthday which was finally adjudicated in a juvenile court or under a youth offender law: (3) any conviction the record of which has been expunged under Federal or State law; and (4) any conviction set aside under the Federal Youth Corrections Act or similar State authority ....

31. While in the military service were you ever convicted by a general court-martial? ....
   If your answer to 30A, 30B, or 31 is "YES", give details in Item 34. Show for each offense; (1) date; (2) charge; (3) place; (4) court; and (5) action taken.

32. Does the United States Government employ in a civilian capacity or as a member of the Armed Forces any relative of yours *(by blood or marriage)? (See Item 32 in the attached instruction sheet)* ....

   If your answer to 32 is "YES", give in Item 34 for such relatives: (1) name, (2) present address (including ZIP Code); (3) relationship, (4) department, agency, or branch of the armed forces.

33. Do you receive, or do you have pending, application for retirement or retainer pay, pension, or other compensation based upon military. Federal civilian, or District of Columbia Government service? ....

   If your answer to 33 is "YES", give details in Item 34. If military retired pay, include the rank at which you retired.

Your Statement cannot be processed until you have answered all questions, including Items 27 through 33 above.
Be sure you have placed an "X" to the left of EVERY marker (◄) above, either in the "YES" or "NO" column.

34, Item No.	Space for detailed answers. Indicate Item numbers to which the answers apply.

If more space is required, use full sheets of paper approximately the same size at this page. Write on each sheet your name, birth date, and announcement or position title. Attach all sheets to this Statement at the top of page 3.

ATTENTION—THIS STATEMENT MUST BE SIGNED
Read the following paragraphs carefully before signing this Statement

A false answer to any question in this Statement may be grounds for not employing you, or for dismissing you after you begin work, and may be punishable by fine or imprisonment (U.S. Code, Title 18, Section 1001). All the information you give will be considered in reviewing your Statement.

AUTHORITY FOR RELEASE OF INFORMATION

I have completed this Statement with the knowledge and understanding that any or all items contained herein may be subject to investigation prescribed by law or Presidential directive and I consent to the release of information concerning my capacity and fitness by employers, educational institutions, law enforcement agencies, and other individuals and agencies, to duly accredited investigators, Personnel Staffing Specialists, and other authorized employees of the Federal Government for that purpose.

CERTIFICATION	SIGNATURE *(sign in ink)*	DATE
I certify that all of the statements made by me are true, complete and correct to the best of my knowledge and belief, and are in made in good faith.		

JIST CARDS

... a taste of your talents

JIST Cards are one of the most powerful, unique, and practical job-search tools being used by job-seekers today. The aim of your JIST Card will be to grab the employer's attention and show at a glance that your skills, abilities, and experiences match up with the employer's expectations.

As you look at the sample JIST Cards on the next page, notice how each card is designed to meet the employer's expectations. Do you see how these cards will show the employer that you are a desirable candidate for an interview and the open position?

Aside from meeting the employer's expectations, your JIST Card also helps you, and the interviewer, in the following ways:

- It effectively answers the questions, *"Tell me about yourself."*

- You appear unique! No two cards look exactly alike or say the same thing.

- It "hooks" the interest of the interviewer . . . quickly.

- Your phone contact (see Chapter 5) comes directly from the information on your JIST Card.

- It shows employers you know what you have to offer.

- Your card allows you to expand on the information during the interview.

- Your confidence level goes up when you can complete and talk about your card.

- Each card shows you are organized and possess important communication skills.

As you prepare your JIST Card, you will be doing an exercise vital to later training. By writing brief statements about your skills, you will develop the vocabulary for speaking with employers. Pay attention! What you do here will affect every part of your job-search.

Sample JIST Cards

John Smith   home (456) 654-1023
         message (456) 963-1742

Vocational Objective: Accounting Clerk/Bookkeeping Or Related Position

Capabilities: Nearly 2 years of related education and work, using similar skills. Graduate of bookkeeping program. Able to maintain accurate financial records, verify and post invoices, inventory, sales, time sheets, etc... Can summarize details, balance books, compile report statistics for planning and tax purposes. Can operate adding machine, electronic bookkeeping equipment and use computerized spread sheets. Well organized, can trouble shoot problems and take instructions well.

Will work various shifts. Attendance record very good.

Honest, Accurate, Detail Minded, Eager Worker With Career Focus

---

Betty Moreno   (356) 543-8759
         (356) 547-3927

Position Of Interest: General Office/Clerical

Knowledge/Skills: 2 years plus actual work, education and volunteer experiences using related skills. Graduate of vocational educational secretarial program (Honors). Can type 50 wpm, operate CRT/wordprocessor, file schedule appointments, generate billings, post receivables, keep time records and respond to customer concerns. Will work with minimal supervision, manage time effectively, make independent decisions and can meet deadline pressures. Careful with office equipment.

Willing to adjust to meet work schedule to meet employer's needs.

Honest, Dependable, Organized, Team Player, Loyal

Sarah Whitaker   Home (812) 654-1764
         Message (812) 647-9214

Employment Objective: Cabinet Making/General Carpentry/Woodworking

Special Skills: Over 5 years of paid/non-paid work and training experience using skills and equipment. Can safely operate joiner/planer, assorted power saws, drill press, lathes, etc.. Can design, build, laminate and install custom orders. Will match materials, complete trim and finish work. Can read blueprints, set trusses and frame. Meet deadlines, cost out and purchase supplies.

Will work until job is correct and will work weekends.

Quality Minded, Career Oriented, Will Work for Every Penny of My Pay

---

David Randolph   home (317) 546-1890
         message (317) 986-7600

Position Desired   Electronics Technician

Skills: Over 3 years of combined and directly related skills, abilities and educational experiences. Vocational school graduate (B +). Can operate Oscilloscope and varied testing equipment, read schematics, design and trouble shoot analog/digital circuitry, basic computer skills. Can logically analyze information, plan and organize daily work, keep accurate/detailed records, follow directions, safety minded and careful with equipment.

Willing to travel, work holidays and weekends, work any shift.

Reliable, Career Minded, Quick Learner, Excited About the Field

---

Juanita Rodriquez   (215) 257-3333
         (215) 632-1190

OBJECTIVE:
Seeking a position on a public relations or business communications staff.

SKILLS:
Able to research, write, and edit news releases, news and feature articles, and advertisements. Capable of designing and preparing brochures and pamphlets.

EXPERIENCE:
Have developed journalism background by working on two high school publications, doing market research, and interning on a magazine. Degree: A.B. Journalism, Indiana University, 1981.

STRENGTHS:
Am creative, responsible, co-operative, organized, and honest.

MAKING YOUR JIST CARDS

In pencil, enter information on your own practice JIST Card on the following page. Don't jump ahead. Complete each section as it is presented throughout this chapter. If you have trouble, refer to the sample JIST Cards on page 71 for ideas. You may want to make a few copies of the practice JIST Card before you begin this exercise in case you make some mistakes or see ways to improve upon your first attempt.

JIST Card Sections

Every JIST Card has ten parts that you need to consider and develop. These parts are

1. Name and Phone Numbers
2. Target Heading
3. Job Objective
4. Value Heading
5. Experience Statement

6. Educational Statement
7. Job-Related Skills Statement
8. Transferable Skills Statement
9. Problem-Solving Statement
10. Self-Management Skills Statement

Try to identify each of these ten parts in the sample cards on the preceding page. In developing your own JIST Card, it's important that you give serious consideration to each section, follow the directions carefully, and enter your information in pencil. You may want to change it later.

Name and Phone Number(s)

The first step in making your own JIST Card is to tell the employer who you are. Print your name in the *Name* space provided on your JIST practice card. Introduce yourself with your proper name. Do not use nicknames.

After stating your name, tell the employer how to contact you. Print your phone number in the *Home Phone* space on your JIST practice card. If someone is taking messages for you when you are unavailable, enter that person's number into the *Message Phone* space provided. Notice on Sarah Whitaker's sample card on the preceding page that *H* and *M* can be used to signify home and message phone numbers if you wish.

Since an employer may only call once, you can't afford to miss a call. If you do not have a phone, list the number of a reliable friend or relative. Be sure to tell the person that you are expecting calls from employers and leave a JIST Card or two with this person.

Target Heading

Now the employer knows your name and how to contact you. But what do you want? You want a job. Call this to the employer's attention with your *Target Heading*.

The following examples are target headings used by other successful job-seekers through the years. Choose one of these or create your own target heading, then enter the heading neatly on your practice card.

Target Headings		
• Vocational Objective	• Field of Experience	• Job Objective
• Employment Objective	• Work Objective	• Career Objective
• Vocational Target	• Job Target	• Career Focus
• Field of Interest	• Employment Goal	• Employment Focus
• Career Focus	• Career Path	• Career Direction

Your Practice JIST Card

_____   _____
(Name)   (Home Phone)

                                         _____
                                                         (Message Phone)

                        (leave space)

_____   _____
(Target Heading)   (Job Objective)
                                            (leave space)

_____   _____
(Value Heading)   (Experience Statement)

                                         _____

                                         _____

                                         _____

                                            (Education Statement)

                                         _____

                                         _____

                                         _____

                                            (Job-Related Skills Statement)

                                         _____

                                         _____

                                         _____

                                            (Transferable Skills Statement)

                                         _____

                                         _____

                                         _____

                        (leave space)

_____
(Problem-Solving Statement)

_____

                        (leave space)

_____
(Self-Management Skills Statement)

_____

Job Objective Statement

Print the title of the job you want in the *Job Objective* section of your practice card. You may choose to include more than one title. If the jobs that interest you are quite different, consider making a separate card for each position.

Value Heading

A *Value Heading* does just what the name implies. It alerts the employer to your value as a worker. It prepares the employer for the powerful information that will follow on your JIST Card. Under the value heading you will write statements about your experience, education, and skills.

Enter your value heading in the space provided on your practice card. You can either select one of the following examples or make up your own.

<table>
<tr><td colspan="3" align="center">Value Heading</td></tr>
<tr><td>● Proven Experiences</td><td>● Areas of Expertise</td><td>● Achievements</td></tr>
<tr><td>● Experiences</td><td>● Success Patterns</td><td>● Successes</td></tr>
<tr><td>● Proven Value</td><td>● Proven Capabilities</td><td>● Proven Worth</td></tr>
<tr><td>● Related Experiences</td><td>● Related Skills</td><td>● Related Abilities</td></tr>
<tr><td>● Accomplishments</td><td>● Supporting Skills</td><td>● Capabilities</td></tr>
<tr><td>● Knowledge/Skills</td><td>● Special Skills</td><td>● Skills/Experience</td></tr>
<tr><td>● Skills</td><td>● Successful Experiences</td><td>● Background</td></tr>
</table>

Experience Statement

Now tell the employer what you have to offer. On your practice card this information is entitled *Experience Statement*. This part of your JIST Card tells the employer how long you've been using similar or related skills and where those skills were developed and used (paid work experience, unpaid work experience, related training or education, hobbies, etc.). Take a look at the sample cards on page 71 to see how others have developed their experience statements. If you find one you like, use it. Otherwise develop your own experience statement — one that fits you like a glove. This is the most important part of your JIST Card so take your time and be careful.

First show your total experience. This should be the length of time you have spent doing things related to your desired job. On the following form, figure your total experience in months and years.

<table>
<tr><td colspan="3" align="center">Total Related Experience</td></tr>
<tr><td></td><td>Years</td><td>Months</td></tr>
<tr><td>Related paid employment (includes military experience)</td><td>_____</td><td>_____</td></tr>
<tr><td>Related unpaid employment (volunteer work; hobbies; and other informal, related work)</td><td>_____</td><td>_____</td></tr>
<tr><td>Related education and training</td><td>_____</td><td>_____</td></tr>
<tr><td>Total</td><td>_____</td><td>_____</td></tr>
</table>

You may not want to include your experience data if your total related experience is less than six months.

Look at the experience statement on the sample cards, then enter your own experience statement in the spaces provided on your practice card. Be positive but don't exaggerate the truth. You'll have to back up everything you write during the interview.

Education Statement

Employers want to know how your education has prepared you for entering the labor market and doing reliable work. If you are a graduate of a technical or business training program, tell the employer. There's no need to name the school, but you must specify the type of training received and the type of certification or diploma received. Naturally, if you have a good grade point average (B or above), list it. If your average was below B, do not list it.

If you are a vocational/technical/business school graduate with a large number of "hands-on" hours, you may want to indicate how many hours were actually spent in training (*"over 1,500 hands-on hours,"* for example).

If you've taken high school or college courses, or have other degrees or certifications that support your job choice, you might want to list them in this section.

If you are a high school graduate without any further formal education, make sure you mention your diploma. If you have no education that shows your value for the job, skip this section. You'll make up for this minor loss in other sections.

Take a look at your *DataTrakt* booklet, Chapter 1, and the JIST Card samples for ideas on how you want to tell the employer that your education will help you do a good job. Enter your education statement(s) in the appropriate space on your practice card.

Job-Related Skills

The *Job-Related Skills* part of your JIST Card tells the employer whether or not you have the basic skills and knowledge to handle the job for which you are applying. You cannot complete this section unless you know the most important demands of the job. Go back into your "Employer Expectations" chapter and your *DataTrakt* booklet to review the demands of your job objective and to identify those that you consider most important.

Select five or six of your job-related skills that would be considered most important in your doing a good job. Enter them onto your practice card in the job-related skills statement section. If you have trouble, take a look at the samples provided on page 71.

Transferable Skills Statement

In the *Transferable Skills* section you will show employers that you have more than just a working knowledge of the job. You will also show them that you will bring transferable skills to your work. These are important skills that most job-seekers — but not you — forget to mention. Go back through your list of transferable skills on page 23 and 24 to select five or six of your most powerful and important transferable skills, then write them on your practice card.

Problem-Solving Statement

Employers like to know that you are willing to help them solve their problems. Some of the most common problems are listed at the top of the next page.

Common Employer Problems	
• employee turnover	• refusal to work weekends or holidays
• refusal of employees to work overtime	• inability or refusal to follow directions
• poor attendance	• unwillingness to do quality work
• tardiness	• inability to get along with co-workers
• unwillingness to travel	
• unwillingness to relocate	

If you are able to solve any of these problems or other problems for employers, list two or three in the problem-solving statement section of your practice card. Write a positive statement such as "Willing to relocate," or "Will work any shift."

Self-Management Skills

Over 60 percent of all workers who are fired are fired because they cannot get along with their co-workers, supervisors, and customers. For this reason, the *Self-Management Skills* section of your JIST Card is extremely important. This statement is also important because it's the last statement you will make about how you will fit into the job and the company.

From your self-management skills exercise on page 27, select three or four of your self-management skills that would be most important in your doing a good job and getting along with other workers and the boss. Enter these skills on the final line of your practice card.

Appearance and Production

Congratulations! You have just completed your first JIST Card. You now have a special paper tool that sets you apart from most job-seekers. Before making copies, consider making improvements. Do you want separate cards for various positions, added information, or a different "look"?

Since appearance counts for 40 percent of your job-search, it makes sense to consider ways to improve the overall appearance of your JIST Card. The preparation of your JIST Card is not the place to pinch pennies. Here are some tips for producing the most attractive JIST Cards possible.

- **Colors** — Since most of the paper blizzard associated with job-search is black and white, make your card stand out. Consider the use of colors such as buff, beige, light blue, cream, ivory, light yellow, or light gray. These are all conservative business colors that make an impact. As with clothing, "hot" colors, such as red or orange, are never acceptable. Some people even like to use ink colors other than black, such as jet, navy blue, and high-gloss dark brown.

- **Size** — Most people developing JIST Cards use a 3″ × 5″ style. This doesn't mean that you can't use 4″ × 6″ cards.

- **Design** — In this chapter you've learned one way — and one way only — to design your card. This is to make sure that you have all of the needed information. Some people use rounded corners or interior borders. You can select from bold type, expanded type, and alternate print sizes and styles. Whatever you do to give your cards a unique design, type the cards and make sure there are no spelling errors. The Juanita Rodriguez sample card on page 71 shows how you can reorganize your JIST Card to make it look entirely different from the practice card. This is an example of what you can do if you want to spend a bit of extra time and effort.

- **Quality and Cost** — Buy high-quality card stock. If you use the 3″ × 5″ card size, you can make a "master" with five cards typed onto one sheet. This will allow you to obtain 500 copies for the price of 100 . . . not a bad deal! An average price for 500 quick-print cards printed from such a master is about $15 to $20 if you do all of the typing and layout work. Add $5 for typing and $10 for borders and layout if you hire outside help.

- **Do them now** — The sooner you have your JIST Cards, the sooner you can put them to good use. Don't procrastinate. Get your cards printed today.

USING YOUR JIST CARD

You waste time and effort if you visit a company and are not allowed to fill out an application. But, with your JIST Card you can leave the employer with more than a quickly fading memory. Simply leave the JIST Card with the person to whom you have been speaking. The JIST Card functions as a business card or calling card. You may say, *"Thank you very much. But I am really interested in working for this company. Could you please keep this card on file? I will check with you again in a couple of weeks."* In this situation your JIST Card introduces you. It gives the employer a permanent record of your visit, even without an application. Also, it shows your initiative, interest, and motivation.

Check back with the companies where you have left JIST Cards. Each visit will make you more familiar to the employer. Your second visit further emphasizes your interest and motivation. It also gives you a chance to become acquainted with the employer. This could benefit you if you have an interview with that person.

On the second visit you can say you have new information to add to your JIST Card. This will let you see if your card has been filed. If it has, print the date you will be available to begin work. If your card has not been filed, write the date on another JIST Card and offer it. If the first was **not** filed, the second one probably will be filed. (Do not, however, make a "pest" of yourself. Appearing overly eager may irritate employers.)

When given an application, fill it out. **Never** use the JIST Card in place of an application. Rather, attach your card to the **upper-right-hand** corner of your application with a paper clip or staple. This will set your application apart from the others. Carry some paper clips or a small stapler with your JIST Cards.

Give a JIST Card to each of your references. These people will be able to use the information on your JIST Card to give you good recommendations. Also give one to each of your friends and relatives and be sure to enclose one with each thank-you note that you send to interviewers. Some job-seekers have even posted their JIST Cards on grocery store bulletin boards.

Remember the skills and good-qualities statements on your JIST Card. They are especially useful when you talk about yourself to employers. They are effective phrases when making telephone contacts and doing interviews. With these phrases you will be able to answer questions such as, *"Why should I hire you?"*

Be generous and creative with your JIST Cards throughout your job-search. They will draw an employer's attention to **you.** Thus, they increase your chances of being chosen for an interview.

HELLO, MY NAME IS HAROLD WATSON. I'M INTERESTED IN A POSITION AS AN INVENTOR'S ASSISTANT. I HAVE SEVERAL YEARS OF EXPERIENCE IN TIN-CAN-AND-TAUT-STRING COMMUNICATIONS SYSTEMS...

WHEN MAY I COME IN FOR AN INTERVIEW AND WITH WHOM WILL I BE SPEAKING?

COME HERE, WATSON. I NEED YOU!

5

TELEPHONE CONTACTS
... dialing for dollars

Only about 25 percent of all available jobs are "visible." These are the jobs that are advertised in newspapers and listed with employment agencies. The average job-seeker goes no further. You, however, already know about paper tools that set you apart from the competition. You can also learn how to uncover the job openings that are not made public. These "hidden" jobs are the real gold mine of job-seeking, making up 75 percent of all available jobs. In this chapter you will learn an effective way to hunt for this gold mine.

Since so few job openings are made public, you cannot wait to hear about them. Check with the companies you are interested in, whether they have listed openings or not.

One way to contact companies is to visit as many as possible each day. Do you think this would be the most efficient use of your time and effort? No, it would not. You would spend too much time traveling and waiting to see people. You would also find it hard to get past all of those receptionists who try to turn away job-seekers. Your JIST Card would help in these situations, but you need to talk to the people who do the hiring. Otherwise, your visits will not be ideal contacts.

A more efficient way to approach employers is to use the telephone. Using the telephone in your job-search provides the following advantages:

- You can contact many employers in just a few hours each day.
- You can gather information faster and easier.
- You are more likely to contact the person doing the hiring.
- You will know better what to expect when you go for an interview.
- You will save money.

In this chapter you will learn to construct and use an important verbal tool — the *telephone contact.* You will construct a phone presentation that will help you get the interviews you want. Your telephone contacts will also produce information that will help you in your job-search.

Your telephone contact will be a brief statement. It will describe who you are, the position you want, and what you have to offer. At the end of the contact you will ask for an interview. Your presentation will meet the three major employer expectations:

- Your **appearance** will be good because you will sound like the kind of person who can do the job.

- You can tell the employer that you are **dependable.** You can also mention other qualities that you have to offer.

- You will be informing the employer about your **skills**.

Your JIST Card will help you construct a telephone presentation. By now you should have your printed JIST Cards. Keep a JIST Card handy as you learn the mechanics of telephone contacts.

A good way to start learning how to construct and use your own phone contact is to listen to how one might sound. The phone contact that follows is based on a JIST Card used as an example in the previous chapter. Notice that the content is similar to John Smith's JIST Card (page 71), but it has been changed to sound as though John were speaking. When you read the contact, imagine that John is calling someone whose name was given to him by a friend. John does not know this person, and there may or may not be a job available.

> *"Hello, my name is John Smith. I'm interested in a position as an accountant or bookkeeper. I'm a graduate of a bookkeeping program and have over two years of combined experience in the accounting field. My skills include processing and posting inventory, sales, payables, payroll, and other accounting functions. I am also able to maintain a general ledger, compile special reports, prepare taxes, and use all standard accounting equipment, including computerized systems. I am organized, reliable, and good at solving problems. When may I come in for an interview?"*

How did that sound? If you were the person being called, would you be impressed? If you hired people with the kinds of skills John has, would you agree to see him?

Most people are impressed by a phone contact such as the one above. Some people think that it sounds pushy, but most people say that John sounds organized and qualified for the job. Most people would be willing to interview John if they had an opening for someone with his skills.

THE BASIC PARTS OF A TELEPHONE CONTACT

A complete, successful telephone contact has four basic parts:

- The **Name** — who you are
- The **Position** — what you want
- The **Hook** — what you have to offer
- The **Goal** — an interview

Let's take a closer look at how each part is constructed.

The Name

When you talk to someone for the first time, you usually greet the person and introduce yourself. This is common courtesy. When you are making telephone contacts, introducing yourself is not only courteous, it is essential. Employers do not like phone calls from nameless strangers. You want potential employers to notice you. Begin each contact with a greeting and your name.

The common greeting below is recommended for your first telephone contacts. Write your first and last name in the space.

"Hello, my name is _____

Always remember to give both your first and last names. Do not start the contact on a first-name basis. You are not making a casual call. Everything you say should prove to the employer that you "mean business."

The Position

After you introduce yourself, tell the employer what you want. Do not force the potential employer to guess the reason for your call. You want a job. Be specific but tactful in stating your desire for a job.

The statement below is recommended for your first telephone contact. Write the job title of the position you want in the blank. Then read the statement aloud to see if it suits you.

"I am interested in a position as a(n) _____

Notice, the word *position* is used in the first example rather than *job*. This is a tactful way of saying what you want. The employer's response to the word *job* would likely be defensive. Never make statements such as the following:

"I'm calling about a job."

"I wonder if you have any jobs?"

"Do you have a job for me?

Little things like this make a difference. If you doubt it, make five calls using the recommended statement and five using the word **job**. Compare the results.

The Hook

The hook may be the most important part of your phone presentation. The hook is a brief statement of your experience and skills. This is what "hooks" the employer and makes him or her want to listen to you. Your hook will set you apart from most applicants who simply ask for *"just any job"* and mention no qualifications.

Your hook should show **action.** Tell the employer what you have done. Then emphasize what you can do and can offer. The following statements are two examples of hooks.

Machinist: *"I have two years' experience as a machinist's helper. I can operate various drill presses, punch presses, lathes, and saws. I am very accurate and a hard worker."*

Beginner: *"I'm dependable, healthy, eager to learn, and I believe in doing good honest work for my wages."*

To make your own hook, use the skills and experience statements from your JIST Card. These statements should already be brief and complete. You need only to put them into a conversational form.

For example, the following hook is based on the JIST Card to the right. *"I have one year of experience working on American and foreign-made cars. I can use all hand and power tools. I am expert in tune-ups, good with customers, and exact in handling cash sales. You will find me reliable, prompt, and willing to learn."*

John Page	(317) 555-1212

POSITION WANTED: Automobile Mechanic

SKILLS: 1 year experience working with American and foreign made cars, can use all hand and power tools, expert in tune-ups. I am good with customers and exact in handling cash sales.

Prefer full-time work

Reliable, Prompt and Willing to Learn

Read the skills and experience parts of your JIST Card aloud. You may want to change some of the wording as you read. When you are comfortable with the sound of your hook, write your hook below.

My Hook

_____

_____

_____

_____

_____

_____

_____

The Goal

Your primary goal for each phone contact is to get an interview. How you state your goal will depend on whether or not you know the person you are calling and whether you have been referred by someone or have simply found this person's name in the phone book. The methods you use to handle each situation will be reviewed in detail later in this chapter.

Remember what John Smith said in the sample phone contact used earlier: *"When can I come in for an interview?"* This question is short, direct, and clear. There is no doubt about what John wants — an interview. You will use similar statements in your phone contacts.

Getting an interview will always be the main goal of your phone contact, but there are actually three additional goals: **referrals, information** and **help**. At the top of the next page — in order of importance — are the four goals for every phone contact.

- **Main Goal: AN INTERVIEW** — Always ask three times, if necessary! If no jobs are open now, ask to interview for future ones. If the person is too busy to see you, offer to see the person the following week, or as soon as it is convenient. If the person is unwilling to set up an appointment now, ask if it is okay to check back, then set a date and time to check back. And call back as promised!

- **GOAL #2: A REFERRAL** — If you can't get an interview, try to get a referral. Ask if the person knows anyone else, either in that same organization or in any other organization, who might use someone with your skills.

- **GOAL #3: INFORMATION** — If you can't get an interview or a referral, try to get useful information about the person's organization, or similar organizations; how to get started in your field; and how you might improve your presentation.

- **GOAL #4: HELP** — Get more help from your contact later and ask for a critique, such as *"Do I sound like a person who would fit into this field if you were hiring?"* You can also ask *"Can I call back for more help later if I need it?"*

YOUR TELEPHONE CONTACT

Based on what you have learned so far, write out your own phone contact in the spaces below. Remember to base your contact on your own JIST Card.

My Phone Contact

Name: *"Hello, my name is* _____ *."*

Position: *"I'm interested in a position as a(n)* _____ *."*

Hook: _____

_____

_____

_____

_____

_____

_____

_____

_____

Goal: _____

_____

You may have to write out your own phone contact several times before it sounds right. Read it out loud after you have written it down. Does it sound natural? Have you written it the way you would speak? Keep making changes until it sounds just right.

If you have trouble perfecting your phone contact, ask your instructor or a friend for help. Rehearse your presentation with friends and family. The more you say it aloud, the more natural it will sound and feel to you.

Many people are shy about saying their contact out loud because it sounds "too good." If this is true for you, ask yourself, *"Is everything I say in this phone contact true? Can I prove it?"* If you can, you must become comfortable with saying these good things about yourself.

You will need to use good judgment about asking when you should offer to call back rather than asking for an interview. Role-playing your phone contact will help you develop a good sense of the best strategy for each case.

Be sure you learn to ask for an interview at least three times before accepting *"No."* You will be amazed how often *"No"* turns to *"Yes"* when you ask that third time.

Send thank-you notes to anyone who is at all helpful. Insert a JIST Card and a resume, and plan to recontact anyone who seems to be a possible employer.

30 Seconds — Count!

Your telephone contact is designed to quickly attract an employer's attention to you and your special qualifications. As you practice your contact, time yourself. You should be able to deliver your full presentation in thirty seconds. Do not rush; be natural.

If you find that you are being interrupted a lot, you need more practice. Pauses in your presentation give the employer a chance to say, *"Sorry, no openings."* You do not want the employer to speak until you have stated your name, position, hook, and goal.

At first it may be obvious that you are reading your telephone contact. Do not be too concerned. Your contact will become more natural the more you use it.

Vim and Vigor

How interested are you in getting a job? Do you really want to work? Your answers may show how enthusiastic you are about getting a job. Enthusiasm is important. It will be reflected in your voice as you make your phone contacts.

Knowing and practicing your basic phone contacts will increase your confidence. However, you must show your spirit with your voice. If you sound uninterested, you will probably get an equal response. If you sound sad, the employer may feel sympathetic. Sadness, however, does not qualify you for a job. With vim and vigor in your voice, you will sound like the person interested in doing the best job.

Practice your presentation in front of a friend. Ask how you sound. If possible, record your telephone contact on a tape recorder. Listen to the recording and decide whether or not you sound convincing. If you do not have a tape recorder, you might borrow one from a friend or the public library.

Some Things to Remember

When making a telephone contact, be brief and to the point. Sound businesslike, but do not be abrupt. Do not let the employer interview you on the phone. Very few people are hired over the phone.

Always your objective is to talk to the most knowledgeable people in the field — the bosses and the employers. Your objective is to get an interview. Failing that, you want to learn as much as you can about your field — and should say so.

Do not address the person you are calling by his or her first name. Using the first name may make the person uncomfortable. It may also give the impression that you are too aggressive or too casual.

If you are calling from home, keep background noise to a minimum.

When you get an appointment for an interview, always repeat the time, day, and date of the interview. Also repeat the interviewer's name, and write down everything!

ADVANCED PHONE TECHNIQUES

Having now mastered your basic phone contact, you can benefit from learning some of the finer points of contacting employers by phone. The remaining parts of this chapter provide helpful tips for making successful phone contacts.

Telephoning Your Friends and Relatives

Among the best sources of job leads are the people you know. You will open your phone contacts with these people more informally than you will open contacts with people you don't know. If the person you are calling knows you well, you might say, *"Hi, this is Jane Marrin* (use your own name here, of course)." You will probably make small talk for a while, then, as soon as possible, get to the point. If the person you are calling does not hire people with your skills, present your hook as you wrote it and ask the person if he or she knows of anyone who might be able to help you. Since your contacts very often will not know anyone, ask another question, such as, *"Do you know anyone else who might know someone who does need a worker with my skills?"* Often this question will produce a name even if the first question didn't.

Getting to the Person Who Can Hire You

In Chapter 7 you will learn more about asking your friends and relatives to help you obtain interviews. You will also learn more about going directly to employers to ask for interviews. Much of what follows in this chapter assumes that you are contacting employers whom you do not know. It is best to be referred to these employers by someone who knows them, but this is not always possible. The techniques for finding which employers to contact will be reviewed in Chapter 7. For now, assume that you have taken the names from the Yellow Pages of the phone book.

Your primary goal is to get an interview. Ideally you want to speak to the person who can both interview and hire you. Ask to speak to that person before you begin your phone contact.

Perhaps you know the name of the supervisor for the job you want. You may have learned it from family or friends. Or, you may have called the company, and asked, *"Who is in charge of the _____ department?"* If you know that person's name, use it. Say, *"Hello, I would like to speak with* (person's name)."

If you do not know the name you need, ask to speak to the right person by *title*. Most companies are organized into departments or units. A manager, supervisor, or director is in charge of a particular department. Ask to speak with that person. You can say, *"Hello, I would like to speak with the manager, please. Could you tell me that person's name?"* Or you can say, *"Hello, I wish to speak to the supervisor of the _____ department. Tell me, what is the supervisor's name?"* Once you reach the right person, give your presentation.

If possible, avoid the personnel department. Most applicants either ask to speak to someone in personnel or they are automatically transferred to personnel because they say, *"I'm looking for a job."* The personnel department has many more applicants than jobs. Therefore, it rejects more applicants than it accepts. You do not want to be screened out. If your call *is* routed to personnel, however, follow through with your presentation.

Each phone contact will test your presentation. If you are constantly interrupted, practice more. If you are getting interviews, you will probably be offered a job soon.

The Secretary Keeps Asking Why You Are Calling

When you make a phone contact, you will usually speak to a secretary or receptionist first. The secretary cannot hire you, so ask for the person who can. Most secretaries will then ask what business you have with that person. How will you state your business?

If you have been referred to this employer by someone who knows the employer, you can simply say something like, *"I was referred to Mr. Jones by a friend of his, Ann Rhodes, who suggested that Mr. Jones could help me."* This technique will usually get you through to the person you want to talk to.

If you have not been referred to an employer by someone the employer knows, consider the following techniques:

- Tell the secretary that you are seeking a position with the company. This is true. However, your call may be channeled to the personnel department rather than to the person you want.

- Say that your business is *personal.* This is true, and will likely get you to your connection. Although this technique works, some employers may see it as a trick and not like it. If they take your call and then find out that they do not have a personal relationship with you, they may form a lasting negative impression of you.

- Be creative. Call to discuss an issue important to the employer. Someone applying for a job as secretary might make the following creative statement: *"I'm calling in reference to current clerical staffing patterns."* Another example: *"I'm calling in respect to methods of increasing administrative support for line staff."*

Whatever reason you give for wishing to speak to the right person, sound businesslike. You will be less apt to get the "runaround."

Shotgunning and Throw-Away Calls

If you still have trouble contacting the right person, try *shotgunning.* With this method you use your presentation on each person with whom you talk. In this way you avoid asking for specific people. You also avoid questions about why you are calling.

Shotgunning depends on the element of surprise. With each person who answers the phone, as fast as 1-2-3-4, you fire off your name, position, hook, and goal. Bang! You confront each person with the unexpected — a job-seeker with a dynamite presentation. These people will have to react.

If you choose this method, chances are you will sometimes be routed to personnel. However, some people will connect you with the person with whom you wish to speak. Why? Simply because you have not called to ask if somebody, somewhere, could give you just any kind of job. Rather, you have presented yourself as a unique person with something to offer.

Another good reason for using shotgunning is that small organizations usually do not have a personnel office. It is often very easy to get to the hiring authority.

When you use shotgunning, do the following:

- Use your basic phone contact on everyone.

- Write down the name of each person with whom you speak. You will then be prepared if you must retrace your steps. If names are not volunteered, ask.

- If you are routed to the personnel department, give your presentation. It is a gamble, but you have nothing to lose. Perhaps there is an opening. If not, you will have gained helpful practice.

After you have memorized your presentation, the best practice is to make *throw-away* calls. Throw-away calls are those in which the outcome is not important. Call the organization lowest on your list of possible employers. If you do not get an interview, you will not be disappointed. If you do get an interview, you will have an opportunity to practice your interview. You might just get an offer for a job!

"Sorry, No Openings"

During your presentation someone may say, *"Sorry, no openings."* The secretary may say it, or the employer — it doesn't matter. What does matter is how you react. Average job-seekers quit here. If someone tells you there are no openings after you have given your phone contact, show that person that you merit a second look. Consider the following examples.

Response #1 to *"Sorry, No Openings"*

"I am very interested in working for your company. When may I call back concerning the position I want?" This shows your motivation and persistence. It compliments the employer's company. It gives you another chance. Get a specific date; a time is optional. Write down the date. Then call back as scheduled.

Response #2 to *"Sorry, No Openings"*

"I am sure my skills will apply to other positions. What positions are available? When may I come in to discuss this with you?" This demonstrates your flexibility, initiative, and knowledge of what you can do.

Response #3 to *"Sorry, No Openings"*

"I understand that there are no openings now, but I would still like to interview with you for future positions that might open up." Remember that your primary goal in making the phone contact is to get an interview. Do not take your first *"No"* as an acceptable answer. Very often if you ask again for an interview after a first or even second *"No,"* you will get an interview.

Response #4 to *"Sorry, No Openings"*

If you do not get an interview after asking several times, you can always ask something like this: *"Do you know of any companies similar to yours that would be interested in a person with my skills?"* This shows your initiative and motivation. It may also get you valuable job leads. When someone tells you about other companies, ask for names of persons to contact.

These responses may be used separately or in combination. Practice saying them aloud. One of these questions could turn a dead-end call into a productive call.

Follow Up!

Following up on your phone contacts can make the difference in whether or not you get a job. Following up is necessary in the two situations described below.

When you get an interview

If you get an interview, make sure you know the name of the person who will be interviewing you. You must also know the correct date, time, and address. Unless the interview is within the next several days, send a thank-you note, a JIST Card, and a resume to help the interviewer prepare for the interview. Send these paper tools the same day that you get the interview.

When you don't get an interview

If you don't get an interview because the key person was busy when you called, and you said you would call later, send a thank-you note! Thank that person for his or her interest, and enclose a JIST Card and resume. Also send a thank-you note if someone referred you to someone or even if someone refused to see you for any reason. It is just good manners to thank people who help you. It is also true that people are far more likely to remember you when jobs open up if you have taken the time to thank them. If you sent your JIST Card along with a thank-you note, they will have your phone number when they need it.

Getting an Interview

If you construct your phone contact with care, and practice it well, you will probably be called in for an interview. Do **not** interview over the phone. Be prepared, however, to answer and ask certain questions during your phone contacts. Here are three areas in which you should be prepared. Write your answers in the spaces provided.

Briefly expand on the skills you have already presented:

_____

_____

_____

_____

Briefly expand on why you would be a good employee:

_____

_____

_____

_____

What questions do you have about the company and the job you are seeking? (Your answer to this question shows your interest and motivation, while making you more informed. However, do **not** ask about pay at this time).

_____

_____

_____

_____

Avoid being caught in a telephone interview. Answer basic questions. Then say, *"Perhaps we could discuss my qualifications further — when I come in for an interview."* If all goes smoothly, the employer will react to you rather than you to him. Thus, an interview will be scheduled. Be sure to write down the interviewer's name, and the address, date, and time of the interview.

Now, **practice** your basic telephone contact. Also practice what you will say when the employer wants to interview you or questions you on the phone.

Overcoming Fears

Making phone contacts is hard for most people. Most people are afraid they will make someone mad or embarrass themselves.

The truth is, however, that most employers like to get phone calls such as the contact you will be making. If you handle your contact well, very little time is wasted and the employers are often impressed enough to offer you an interview. Smart employers are always willing to meet people with the skills the employers need to run their businesses or organizations. They are often willing to see you even when they have no openings! They will do this to consider you for the future, help you out with a referral, or give you other support.

Experience with phone contacts has shown that it takes from ten to fifteen calls to get one interview. This means that you will hear the word *"No"* more than the word *"Yes."* While this may sound discouraging at first, consider that you can easily make ten phone calls an hour. At that rate you can often get two interviews in just a few hours. If you did this every day, you would have ten interviews a week, or forty a month. You will get a job very quickly if you get this many interviews.

You will discover that very, very few employers will be rude to you. Perhaps one in a hundred. The rest will be polite, even if they do not agree to interview you right away. If you send thank-you notes to these people and follow up with them later, you will be surprised at how often *"No"* will later become *"Yes."* It's that simple.

YOU'VE GOT THE JOB!

CHECK LIST
+ Appearance
+ Dependable
+ Personality
+ SKILLS
+ Knowledge

the WORK BOOK

6

THE INTERVIEW

... for rave reviews

Doing well in a job interview is essential to getting most jobs. Very few people are hired without first being interviewed. The time you spend interviewing is the most important time in your job-search.

In a typical situation, the interviewer will be considering a number of people for one job. The interviewer will need to eliminate everyone from consideration except the one person who is eventually hired. This means that the interviewer will try to find weaknesses in each applicant.

If this sounds unfriendly, it is! Keep in mind that an interview is really a business transaction. You offer something of value (your effort) in exchange for money (the employer's job opening). There is more to it than this, of course, but value for pay is the basis of the hiring decision.

Interviews last from fifteen minutes to well over an hour. Most last thirty to forty-five minutes. If you aren't screened out in the first interview, you will often be asked to a second or even a third interview before you are offered a job.

Job interviews usually end in one of three ways:

- The employer offers the applicant a job.

- The employer rejects the applicant, or the applicant rejects the job.

- No decision is made until a future date. This is the most common of the three results.

You will have several great advantages over most job-seekers. You know what employers look for in the people they hire, and you know enough about yourself to tell employers what you have to offer. In this chapter you will learn how you can meet the three main employer expectations in your interviews.

APPEARANCE

Do you look like the right person for the job?

Do you remember the four aspects of good appearance? They are the way you *look, behave, write,* and *speak*. In an interview you can show each of these aspects of appearance, or your appearance can quickly make a negative impression. If you do make a bad impression, you may never get the chance to present your skills or abilities to do the job well. First impressions are very important — you want to make the most positive first impression you can make.

The Way You Look

Refer to page 11 to see what you will be wearing to the interview. Start preparing your personal appearance the night before an interview. Get your clothing ready. You will then have one less concern at the last moment. Preparing your clothes the night before will help you follow the basic rules of dress for an interview.

Dressing Rules for an Interview

- Dress one step above what you would actually wear on the job.
- Never wear jeans, a T-shirt, or tennis shoes to an interview.
- Dress in clothing that is clean, neat, and in good condition.
- Dress conservatively!

The second part of personal appearance is good grooming. Good grooming is required for **all** interviews. Good grooming shows employers that you value yourself and are likely to be proud of your work.

Like careful dressing, good grooming starts the night before an interview. Anything you can do the night before saves you time at the last moment. Which of the following could you do the night before?

Good Grooming Checklist

- Trim, clean, comb, and neatly style your hair.
- Men must shave. Neatly comb and trim mustaches and beards. Take an honest look at yourself. Is there enough there to really call it a beard or mustache? If not, shave it off. You may grow it again after you have your job.
- Neatly trim your fingernails. Women who use nail polish should choose a conservative color.
- Apply any makeup, perfume, or after-shave lotion sparingly.
- Be sure your clothing is clean, pressed, and in good condition.

Last, but not least, is the hygiene part of your personal appearance. Good hygiene should be a habit, but review the basic rules once more.

Rules for Hygiene

- Good personal hygiene always begins with a clean body — bathe thoroughly.

- Shampoo your hair.

- Brush your teeth. (If you chew gum, dispose of the gum before an interview.)

- Use deodorant.

- Clean your fingernails.

Remember — 40 percent of the job-seekers who stay unemployed do so because their personal appearance does not meet employer expectations. If just one part of your personal appearance is neglected, the employer will probably not think that you are the right person for the job.

The Way You Behave

The second part of appearance is the way you act. At an interview you will be observed from the moment you enter the door. Walk in with confidence and energy. Greet the secretary or receptionist with a smile. Tell this person your name and the reason you are there. Say, for example, *"Good morning, Ms. Smith. My name is Charles Attwood. I'm here to interview for the assembler position."* Or say, *"Hello. I'm Trisha Conner. I have a 3:00 appointment with Mrs. Ford."*

You should arrive ten to fifteen minutes early. Use this time wisely. Take notice of the surroundings. Look for reading material. Do not pace the floor. Be calm and look smart. The employer may not be watching you, but the secretary probably is. The secretary might describe your waiting-room manner to the employer.

When you are called in for your interview, greet the employer with a firm handshake and a smile. Be ready with an opening statement. An example would be *"Good day Mr. Jones. My name is Charles Attwood."* Never use the employer's first name — you are not old friends yet. Do not sit down until the employer offers you a seat. If the employer does not offer one, ask if you may sit down. Sit up straight or lean slightly forward in your chair to show your interest. Keep your feet on the floor and your hands in your lap. Use gestures and body movements to express yourself but do not be extreme. Look the interviewer in the eye to show that you are honest and confident. However, do not stare. If you find it hard to keep eye contact, look at the interviewer's nose or eyebrows.

Always be alert. This shows that you are eager to learn and succeed. Be sure to thank the employer for the time and consideration given you.

The Way You Write

The third aspect of good appearance is the way you write — your paperwork. Your paperwork often needs to meet an employer's expectations before you get an interview. Unless your paperwork is neat, complete, and accurate, you may not be interviewed. Even if you do get an interview, poor paperwork will mean you already have marks against you.

As you know, your paperwork tools are your *DataTrakt*, applications, and JIST Cards. For some, paperwork also includes a resume. (Artists, writers, and photographers may also need samples of their work.)

Paperwork appearance starts with a complete and accurate *DataTrakt*. Be sure to take your *DataTrakt* when you go to an interview. Without it, you will have a hard time preparing an application that meets employer expectations. Also take several JIST Cards and your resume, if you have one. Your paperwork should help you **get** an interview, not **lose** one.

The Way You Speak

Most employers want to hire workers with good verbal communication skills — for **all** jobs. These employers believe that their businesses will run more smoothly and more profitably if their workers can communicate effectively. They want workers who do the following when they speak:

- pronounce words clearly and confidently so that everyone can understand
- speak in complete, logical sentences so that there is no doubt about the meaning of what's being said
- show enthusiasm and spirit when they talk
- use correct grammar
- speak honestly and openly, rather than "beating around the bush" or avoiding tough questions

If you are weak in any of the areas listed above, work on improving the appearance you make when you speak. In many interviews the way you talk about your skills and experiences will be just as important as the skills and experiences themselves.

DEPENDABILITY

Can you be counted on to do the job?

Remember that the second employer expectation concerns your dependability. You may be asking, *"How can I show this in my interview?"* Of course, you can show it just by showing up for your interview. You can show that you are punctual by being on time.

Tell the interviewer that you are dependable and punctual. Always support your statements. For example, say, *"I am a well-organized person. I have always been on time in coming to work, keeping my appointments, and turning in my reports. Punctuality is very important to me and I'm proud of my record."* Or you can say, *"My last employer used to laugh and say he didn't need a watch to tell what time it was because I always walked through the door at 7:45."*

In Chapter 1 you listed examples and wrote some statements to express your good attendance, punctuality, and reliability. Pick the best examples, then rewrite them and your statements below. Make any improvements in your statements that you can think of. The *proof-by-example* technique described on page 94 may help you. Use additional pages if you need them.

Attendance Statement: _____

_____

Example: _____

_____

Punctuality Statement: _____

_____

    Example: _____

_____

Dependability Statement: _____

_____

    Example: _____

_____

SKILLS

What can you do that relates to this job?

    Interviewers want to know if your skills qualify you for a certain job. They are looking for someone with the right skills and qualifications, and the ability to learn the necessary new skills. Interviewers ask questions to find out about your skills. However, some things will not be covered unless you mention them. You have a lot to offer the employer. It is up to you to say so during the interview. Now is a good time to review previous chapters and your job-seeking tools. You should find several well-organized lists of your most relevant skills.

    It is important that you make several different skills statements during an interview. You must do this to let your interviewer know you are the right person for the job. Make your skills statements positive. Tell how you used your skills in former positions. (Remember, one small bit of negative data carries more weight than a huge piece of positive information.)

    Talk about your skills early in the interview. Do this in as many different ways as possible. Remember — employers tend to make decisions within the first four to nine minutes. If you compile a group of skills statements, you will have a powerful message for those first, critical minutes of the interview.

    As an exercise, assemble your strongest skills statements from this book and from your job-seeking tools. Consider how you might improve the statement as you write them here. Always be complete, accurate, and positive. Remember that each statement must relate to the job for which you are applying. If a statement does not apply, list another skill instead.

Job-Related Skills Statement: _____

_____

_____

Transferable Skills Statement: _____

_____

_____

Self-Management Skills Statement: _____

_____

_____

By now you should know which of your qualifications best relate to the job you want. You should be able to present your qualifications as answers to an interviewer's questions. The best way to sort and assemble your data is to relate it to questions an interviewer will probably ask. The true test of your skills statements will be how well you meet employer expectations in the face of difficult questions.

PROOF-BY-EXAMPLE

Proof-by-example is an important interview strategy. It will provide you with an easy way to give powerful responses to almost any interview question. Without knowing it you've actually been using the proof-by-example technique since Chapter 1, when you learned about the importance of using specific examples to support all of your skills and experience statements.

Suppose someone is asked the following question in an interview: *"Why don't you tell me about yourself?"* Most job-seekers do not handle this question well. Here's how a person using the proof-by-example approach might answer the question:

> *"Well, you probably want to know what sort of worker I am. I am the kind of person who finishes things I start. I get a great deal of satisfaction from knowing that I have done something well and that I did it on time. For example, in a previous job I was given the responsibility of finishing an important project after another person left the company. I had to stay up nights reviewing the procedures and revising the plans for a job our company was bidding on. All of this was new to me, but I finished the project on time and we were awarded a project worth over one million dollars. I feel I can use the same skills and hard work to do well on this job, too."*

Sounds good, doesn't it? Let's break down this person's response so that we can look at it more closely. This process will help you learn how to make proof-by-example responses.

In learning how to use proof-by-example more effectively, you should assign points to the proof-by-example steps, as shown below. A score of "10" is the highest possible score for any one response — it means that you have done an excellent job in developing a solid interview answer.

Points

1. **Provide a good example of a key skill** — By now you know your skills   **1**
   and those needed on the job for which you are interviewing. You
   should also have a variety of examples of where you used these skills.
   Think of one good example you could use to support a skill needed
   to do this job well. Name that skill (in the example above, it was
   "finishing things I start"); then, give a good example of when you used this skill. Try to think of your best examples from previous work
   or other situations. You should have **at least** three examples for each
   skill presented.

2. **Give details** — Provide enough details in your example to make your example an interesting but short story. Tell as much as is necessary about *who, what, where, when,* and *why* for the story to make sense. 1

3. **Use numbers or other measurable data** — People will pay more attention if you use some numbers to support your story. Talk about dollars saved, number of people served, percentage of sales increased, budget per year, or increased orders. Use any numbers or pieces of data that you can think of! 1

4. **Mention results** — Did your work accomplish the intended purpose? How do you know? Tell how you know. 2

5. **Link and think** — Look for a way to connect what you did in your example to doing a good job in the position for which you are interviewing. The more specific you can be, the better. 5

_____

Total   10

You can improve your interviewing skills by simply scoring your responses in terms of how well they meet the five steps in the proof-by-example strategy. Give yourself the proper number of points for each part you include in your own interview responses. How many points would you give the response used in the example above?

PROBLEM QUESTIONS

A problem question is a question that the average job-seeker would find difficult to answer in a **positive** way. You should expect several problem questions in each interview. However, no question will pose a real problem if you are prepared to answer it. In fact, most interview questions should help you tell how you meet the employer's expectations.

Understanding which employer expectation is actually behind a problem question will help you make the best possible answer to the question. For example, if the interviewer asks why you left your last job, the interviewer is probably trying to find out whether or not you are dependable. Knowing this will help you answer the question in a way that says you will meet that employer expectation. You might say, *"I left my last job because I decided that my long-term career goal was to be a _____. I took several classes to prepare myself for the change in jobs and saved for many months to prepare for a full-time job-search. I know I did the right thing and am looking forward to a position in this field."*

Whatever your situation, you must find ways to present yourself in the most positive way. When the facts are not positive, it is best to be honest, and then quickly present what you learned from that situation to help you do well in this job.

To prepare for interviews you must become familiar with the typical questions. The following pages contain lists of the common interview questions. Any question could pose a problem. You must be able to respond quickly and positively. Note any question that is difficult for you to answer. Think about, write down, and then practice presenting positive answers to both the easy questions and the hard ones.

This first list includes some of the most common interview questions that job-seekers often have trouble answering.

"Won't you tell me about yourself?"

"Why have you held so many jobs?"

"What is your major weakness?"

"How much do you expect to be paid?"

"Why do you want to work for this company?"

"Why did you leave your last job?"

"Why do you have this gap in your job history?"

"What are your future plans?"

"What do you like to do in your leisure time?"

These questions are commonly asked in job interviews. Consider each separately.

"Won't you tell me about yourself?"

This may be one of the interviewer's first questions. The interviewer is not trying to un-cover your personal problems or love life. This question is asked to find out about your job skills. It also allows the interviewer to see how well you express yourself. There are several similar questions.

"Why should I hire you?"

"What is your experience?"

"Tell me about other jobs you have had."

Be prepared to give the entire series of statements about your best qualifications for the job. Be specific and include examples to support your claims. With every response, try to show that you meet one or more of the three major employer expectations. Before responding to the question in the exercise space below, you may want to review the examples in Chapter 1.

Now take the time to make your own response as complete, accurate, and positive as possible. Note that the question lets you talk about your dedication to attendance, punctuality, and dependability, as well as your skills. Use the five-step, proof-by-example approach. Ready?

Employer: *"Won't you tell me about yourself?"*

Your Response: _____

_____

_____

_____

_____

_____

"Why have you held so many jobs?"

The average person under the age of thirty-five changes jobs every one-and-a-half years. People over thirty-five take new jobs every three years.[1] With this in mind, have you had an unusual number of jobs? If not, you may never be asked the question. If an interviewer does ask why you have had so many jobs, explain that you have kept your jobs as long as the average, or longer. Assure the interviewer that you intend to stay with this new job for quite some time. Tell the interviewer that this is the job you want and that you can do it well. Emphasize your dependability.

Job-seekers who have had many jobs in a short time tend to follow one of two patterns. In one pattern the job-seekers take different *kinds* of jobs. In the other pattern they do the same kind of job, but change employers often. None of these job-seekers appear dependable. They will all need to give good reasons for leaving their previous jobs.

If you have had many different kinds of jobs, you may have been deciding on a career. A positive reason for your work record could be that **you were exploring different careers.** In your various jobs you have gained skills, abilities, experience, responsibilities, and training that relate to the job you seek. Be prepared with good reasons for having left past jobs. (You will find a list of common reasons for leaving a job on page 34.)

Your work record may show that you have always had the same kind of job, but at different companies. This pattern may suggest that you quit or were fired because of personal problems. Your *DataTrakt* and application should show employers that there were no negative reasons for leaving former jobs. You should support these reasons in the interview, if practical. However, if you think a former employer will speak negatively of you, cover yourself. People are usually fired because personal, nonwork problems interfere with their work. If you must mention a personal problem, be general and brief. Explain that the problem has been resolved. Note in the following examples that negative words, like *fired,* are never used.

> *"I left my job because I was going through a divorce. I went back to work as soon as that problem was completely resolved."*

> *"I had to leave my job because I was experiencing extreme anguish due to the death of my son. I'm ready to begin my life again. I'm ready for work."*

> *"I was involved in an auto accident and had to stay home for several months. After recovering completely, I resumed work."*

> *"A few years back I had a drinking problem and missed some work. However, I joined A.A. and haven't touched a drop in three years now. In my present position I've received two annual bonus checks for perfect attendance."*

After describing your problem and how you resolved it, get right back to outlining your qualifications! Again, emphasize dependability. Respond if this question applies to you. If it does not apply, go to the next section.

Employer: *"Why have you held so many jobs?* _____

Your Response: _____

_____

_____

_____

"What is your major weakness?"

This question is designed to give the interviewer negative information about you. It also tests your ability to handle tough questions. Stick to job-related information. **Never** be negative. Rather, turn any negative issue into a positive statement. Turn your weaknesses into a strength. Show that you are willing to work and to learn new skills. On the following page are some examples of weaknesses stated as positives.

---

[1]Richard N. Bolles, *What Color Is Your Parachute?* (Berkeley: Ten Speed Press, 1986), p. v.

Weakness:	*"I'm slow."*
Positive Statement:	*"I'm often too careful about my work. Sometimes I work late to get my job done just right."*
Weakness:	*"I don't like people telling me what to do."*
Positive Statement:	*"I tend to ask questions about what I am told to do so I can be sure I will do it right."*

Do not tell the interviewer that you have no weaknesses. If you cannot think of one, say something positive about yourself. For example, say, *"Maybe it would be my curiosity about how things work. I like to learn new skills and see how things fit together."*

Now write a positive response to the question, *"What is your major weakness?"*

Your Response: _____

_____

_____

_____

_____

"How much do you expect to be paid?

A poor response to the salary question can turn out to be a very expensive lesson. Unless you are being offered a job, don't talk about salary at all. Whatever you say about money in an early interview will probably screen you out of the job.

Let's say that the employer is willing to pay $10 per hour, but you say you will accept $6. What do you think you will be paid if you get the job? And you should realize that answering *"$6"* in this situation may prevent you from getting the job. The employer may keep looking for a person who thinks he or she is worth more than you think you are worth. It can work just this way!

Your answer can also work against you if you say you are looking for more salary than the interviewer had in mind. The interviewer might just keep looking for a person who would be happy with the salary range the employer has in mind.

You might try a neutral statement that does not commit you either way. For example, say, *"I would expect to be paid what other persons in this job are paid."* Sometimes it is best to answer this question with another question. The simplest replies would be *"How much does the job pay?"* or *"How much is a new employee in this position usually paid?"* If you have experience in the same kind of job, you might say, *"How much do you usually pay someone with my experience?"* Answering the question with a question may get you a salary higher than what you would have received otherwise.

Another good approach is to mention a salary range that probably includes the salary the employer is considering, but also goes higher. For example, if you think the employer will probably pay an annual salary of about $15,000, you might say that you are looking for a salary in the mid-teens to lower twenties. This answer covers a huge range, from $13,000 to $24,000, and should let you move on to more important topics.

Remember, avoid negotiating salary until after you are offered the job.

Which type of response do you think is best for you? Try it out here. *"How much do you expect to be paid?"*

Your Response: _____

_____

_____

_____

"Why do you want to work for this company?"

This question presents a problem only if you do not expect it to be asked. Also, if you are not prepared, you will miss your chance to compliment the company and, thus, the interviewer. The interviewer does not necessarily ask the question to get a compliment. However, your answer should always include a compliment. The interviewer expects you to show your interest. You can do this with an answer that indicates you have researched the company.

Research each company before you go to an interview. You can do this in many different ways. Most research takes very little time. It can make the difference in whether or not you are hired. (See Chapter 7.)

Visit the company. If you know people who work at the company, talk to them. Ask employees with jobs similar to the one you want what they like about the company. This gives you an answer to the interviewer's question. You can say, *"I've talked with some of your employees, and they feel this is a good company to work for because . . ."*

Read company newsletters and financial reports. You can then say, *"I have been reading that your company is really growing fast. I want to work for your company because it has a great future and can offer me a chance to grow."* Write your own answer to the question *"Why do you want to work for this company?"*

Your Response: _____

_____

_____

_____

"Why did you leave your last job?"

The employer asks this question to find out if you had any problems on your last job. If you did, you may have the same problems on a new job. Following are some tips on how to answer this question.

- **Never** say anything negative about yourself or your previous employer. If you did have problems, think of a way to explain them without being negative.

- Be very careful not to use the word *fired* when explaining why you left the previous job. Perhaps you were *laid off* or your position was *cut.* Use these words to explain what happened.

- If you were fired and are not on good terms with your previous employer, maybe you should explain. First examine why you were fired. Try to learn something from the situation. Were you partly to blame?

- If you have learned something from the situation, explain this honestly. Avoid criticizing your employer. The odds are good that the interviewer has been fired at some time too. He or she may understand your situation better than you expect.

Many people are fired because nonwork issues interfere with their work. Did a divorce, car problem, or something else in your personal life cause you to be fired? Have you resolved the problem? If so, let the interviewer know this. Tell the interviewer that the former problem will not affect your work. See page 34 for a list of common reasons for leaving a job. Your *DataTrakt* should also contain reason-for-leaving statements.

Prepare a positive explanation if possible. Practice answering the question, *"Why did you leave your last job?"* Write the best answer below.

Your Response: _____

_____

_____

_____

"Why do you have this gap in your job history?"

Questions about job gaps are very important questions. How you answer these questions is even more important. If you have not been out of work for over two months, don't worry. Statistics show that the average period of unemployment between jobs is over three months.[1] You might point this out to the interviewer. You have been *"looking for work."* However, if you give the interviewer that answer, you probably will not get the job. Obviously you are looking for work. The interviewer wants to know what else you are doing: *"Working part-time?" "Doing volunteer work?" "Getting your house in order?" "Having a much-needed rest?"* All of these answers show that you are an active, thinking person who makes good use of time. Below are some other answers that you may use.

"I decided I was needed at home."

"I went back to being a full-time homemaker."

"I decided to further my education."

"I was in business for myself."

Whatever your reasons for a job gap, you must assure the interviewer that the condition no longer exists and that you are ready to work. The following statement shows how this is done.

"During the past six months I've been self-employed. Now, with the condition of the economy as it is, I find that I need a regular income. I've gotten the desire for self-employment out of my system. I'm ready to work and would like very much to work for your company."

If you have a job gap you need to cover, write your response below.

Your Response: _____

_____

_____

_____

---

[1]United States Department of Labor, Bureau of Labor Statistics, *Employment and Earnings Bulletin*, Vol. 25, No. 1

"What are your future plans?"

There are several reasons for asking this question. The interviewer may want to know if you are ambitious, plan ahead, or if you set goals for yourself. The interviewer may also want to know what kind of expectations **you** have of the company. If you expect too much, you may have morale problems and not stay long. There are no correct answers. However, you should have a good, positive answer prepared.

"How ambitious are you?" An answer might be *"I hope to become very good at my job and perhaps take some schooling to become a top-notch executive secretary."* Another could be *"I intend to learn the stock so well that I can become a buyer for the department."* Both answers tell the interviewer that you want to get ahead and can set realistic goals. They also say that you plan to be around awhile.

Now write your own answer to the question about plans. Emphasize your ambition and use the proof-by-example approach to support your statements.

"What are your future plans?"

Your Response: _____

_____

_____

_____

"What do you like to do in your leisure time?"

Interviewers ask this question to see if your activities and hobbies might help the company. They also want to know if you do more than watch television night after night. This is your chance to mention community and civic groups to which you belong, hobbies, and volunteer work. If you have held a leadership position in a group, be sure to say so.

"What do you like to do in your leisure time?"

Your Response: _____

_____

_____

_____

MORE INTERVIEW QUESTIONS

The interview questions in the prior section are common ones, but especially hard ones. You should be prepared for many other questions. On the following pages are a number of interview questions. You may be asked any of these questions during the course of your job-search. Do not think that these are all of the possible questions. They are simply more tools to help you better prepare for interviews.

Pick out the questions you find especially hard. Then prepare positive answers for them. If you cannot decide which are problem questions, choose the questions you hope the employer does not ask.

When preparing your answers, write them down and save them. Otherwise, you may forget them. Next, practice your answers until they sound and feel right. If you are not comfortable with your answers, rewrite them.

When you are satisfied with your answers, find as many practice interviewers (friends or family members) as possible. Have them choose questions from each section — let them surprise you. Make each practice interview as real as possible. That is, pick a certain kind of company so that your practice interviewer can ask specific questions. Do your practice interviews as if they were real. All interviews start with a handshake and a greeting. Try to meet as many employer expectations as possible. Use proper manners. Your answers should show that you are dependable and punctual. Also, be sure to mention all your related skills and interests. Be sure that the last question your interviewer asks is *"Do you have any questions?"*

Do not let your practice interviewers be too easy on you. Tell them to ask problem questions. They will not help you by being too nice. You cannot count on the real interviewer being easy with you.

Practice, Practice, Practice! The more practice interviews you do, the fewer surprises you will have in the real interviews. The fewer surprises you have, the more employer expectations you will be able to meet. The more employer expectations you meet, the better your chances of getting a job.

As you practice answering the following questions, use the proof-by-example rating system to score your responses from one to five (See page 94). Write your scores on the lines next to the questions. If a question does not relate to you, put a dash in that space. If your scores are low for a particular question, keep working on that question. Also do extra work on any questions you feel are particularly important for you to answer well. Review Chapter 2 and Chapter 3 for more ideas on how to answer these questions.

General Questions

_____ *"What can I do for you today?"*

_____ *"Won't you tell me a little about yourself?"*

_____ *"What is the position for which you are applying?"*

_____ *"How did you learn of this position?"*

_____ *"What kind of work interests you?"*

_____ *"What is your major weakness?"*

_____ *"What qualities are necessary to succeed in this kind of work?"*

_____ *"What do you think might be some of the disadvantages of this kind of work?"*

_____ *"Why do you want to return to work?"*

_____ *"What interests you about our product or service?"*

Training Questions

_____ *"Do you have any special training?"*

_____ *"What machines can you operate?"*

_____ *"Would you prefer on-the-job training or a formal training program?"*

_____ *"What can you do for this company now?"*

_____ *"Are you a veteran? Did you gain any job-related experience in the service?"*

Education Questions

_____ *"Do you have a high school diploma?"*

_____ *"What was your rank in your high school class?"*

_____ *"You have a low grade point average. Why were your grades so poor?"*

_____ *"When and why did you choose your particular major in college?"*

_____ *"Why did you leave college before graduating?"*

_____ *"Did you finance part or all of your eduation? If so, how?"*

_____ *"What type of books have you read?"*

_____ *"What were your extracurricular activities?"*

_____ *"What subject(s) did you most enjoy studying? Least enjoy studying?"*

Family and Friends Questions

_____ *"Are you married?"*

_____ *"Do you have any dependents? If so, how many?"*

_____ *"Do you have child care arranged?"*

_____ *"Who will care for your child when he or she is too ill to go to the sitter or school?"*

_____ *"How would your family feel about your taking long business trips away from home?"*

_____ *"What are the occupations of your parents?"*

_____ *"What was home life like when you were growing up?"*

_____ *"How old were you when you became self-supporting?"*

_____ *"Do you have any major debts?"*

_____ *"How much money do you expect to be making in ten years?"*

Questions Concerning Health

_____ *"Do you have any health problems?"*

_____ *"Have you ever had any serious illness or injury?"*

_____ *"Have you ever been hospitalized?"*

_____ *"Are you taking any kind of medication at present?"*

_____ *"Do you have any disabilities or physical limitations?"*

_____ *"Will your limitations interfere with your job performance?"*

_____ *"How often have you been absent from work or school?"*

_____ *"Do you have any objection to taking some psychological tests?"*

_____ *"Do you have emotional problems? How do they affect you?"*

_____ *"Don't you feel a little too old (or young) for this job?"*

_____ *"To what extent do you use alcohol? Have you ever used illegal drugs?"*

Transportation Questions

_____ *"How would you be getting to work each day?"*

_____ *"Do you have a driver's license?"*

_____ *"How far do you live from here? How much time will it take to get to work?"*

_____ *"Would you mind moving from this area if the company chooses to relocate you?"*

_____ *"Can you do considerable traveling?"*

Availability Questions

_____ *"Do you want to work full-time?"*

_____ *"Would you be available for part-time work?"*

_____ *"What hours would you be available for work?"*

_____ *"What shift do you prefer?"*

_____ *"Will you be available for weekend work?"*

_____ *"Can you work the night shift?"*

_____ *"Will you be available for overtime work?"*

_____ *"We rotate shifts every four months. Would this suit you?"*

Work Experience Questions

_____ *"What kind of job do you want?"*

_____ *"What experience do you have that relates to the job you want?"*

_____ *"What jobs have you held?"*

_____ *"Why have you held so many jobs?"*

_____ *"Could you explain this gap in your job history?"*

_____ *"What did you like most about your last job? What did you like least?"*

_____ *"Why should I hire you?"*

_____ *"How do you know you can do this job?"*

_____ *"What do you know about this particular position?"*

_____ *"What do you know about our company?"*

_____ *"Why do you want to work for this company?"*

_____ *"Do you get along well with people?"*

_____ *"Have you ever had trouble with other people on the job?"*

_____ *"Can you take instructions without getting upset?"*

_____ *"What do you do if you have a personality clash with a supervisor?"*

_____ *"What would you do if you started to become bored with work?"*

_____ *"What if a personal problem interferes with your performance?"*

_____ *"Will you fight to get ahead?"*

_____ *"What have you learned from previous jobs?"*

_____ *"What do you think determines a person's progress in a good company?"*

_____ *"What things have you done that show initiative and willingness to work?"*

_____ *"What supervisory or leadership roles have you held?"*

_____ *"What qualifications do you have for this job?"*

_____ *"Why should you be successful in this position?"*

_____ *"What examples can you give that emphasize your interest in this kind of work?"*

_____ *"Can you list any examples of your creativity?"*

_____ *"Are you a good manager? What examples support your claim?"*

_____ *"Have you ever developed or helped to develop any programs? What? How?"*

_____ *"Have you ever helped to reduce operating costs? How?"*

_____ *"How would you describe your personality?"*

_____ *"What do fellow workers think of you?"*

_____ *"Have you ever hired people before? What do you expect of an employee?"*

_____ *"Have you ever fired anyone?"*

_____ *"Can you work well under pressure?"*

_____ *"Do you like routine work?"*

_____ *"What do you do in your spare time?"*

_____ *"What was your most important accomplishment during your school years?"*

_____ *"What did you learn from part-time or summer job experiences?"*

_____ *"Have you ever been unemployed for two months or longer? Why?"*

_____ *"Why did you quit various jobs you have had?"*

_____ *"Do you have references?"*

_____ *"Would your last employer recommend you?"*

Future Plans Questions

_____ *"What are your plans for the future?"*

_____ *"What would you like to be doing five years from now? Ten years from now?"*

_____ *"In what geographic location would you prefer to live? Why?"*

_____ *"How does this position relate to your career goals?"*

_____ *"How long would you stay with the company if you were offered this job?"*

_____ *"What other positions have you considered?"*

_____ *"What is your philosophy of life?"*

_____ *"Do you plan to go back to school someday?"*

Money and Benefits Questions

_____ *"How much would you expect to be paid?"*

_____ *"What do you expect in terms of benefits?"*

_____ *"What benefits did you receive from your previous employer?"*

_____ *"What was your salary for your last job?"*

Four More Problem Questions

Everyone has a few things they would rather not have to answer. An employer just might ask these very questions. If so, you may have to answer them. What are the four questions an employer might ask you that you would have the hardest time answering? List them below.

1. _____

2. _____

3. _____

4. _____

Now, how could you answer these questions in a positive way? Practice writing your answers on another page. Write your final answers below.

1. _____

_____

_____

2. _____

_____

_____

3. _____

_____

_____

4. _____

_____

_____

ILLEGAL QUESTIONS

You should be considered for a job on the basis of your ability to do that job. Unfortunately not all employers hire people on this basis. Some employers make their decisions for reasons that may not be fair to certain job-seekers. Laws have been passed to give all job-seekers a fair chance at getting a job. There are many opinions on what is legal and illegal for an employer to ask. These laws are subject to change. In this section many of the questions considered illegal have been included. Illegal or not, they may come up in your job-search.

There are several ways to handle what you feel may be an illegal question. One way is to simply point out to the employer that you think the question may be illegal. Even if you can do this humorously, it can result in your losing a potential job offer. Suppose you choose not to answer the question. You may save yourself from working for an employer for whom you would not have wanted to work. You will have to judge this for yourself.

Often an employer intends no harm and is simply a poor or untrained interviewer. In this case it is often best to respond simply and then change the subject. Read the two examples below.

Question: *"Are you married?"*

Answer: *"I'm now divorced. Though painful, my divorce has given me a new sense of commitment to my career."*

Question: *"Who takes care of your children?"*

Answer: *"My children are well cared for. I never miss a workday even when they are ill."*

Notice in the examples above how these questions can be used to meet employer expectations. This is an effective approach that can be made even more effective if followed by the proof-by-example strategy.

If you feel you were not considered for a job because of an illegal question, you may wish to complain to a supervisor. You may want to make a more formal complaint. However, this does not help you get a job. It could also take time away from your job-search.

Here are some of the questions that many people feel are illegal. Be prepared to answer the ones that apply to you in some way. Put a check next to those you can answer quickly and positively.

General

_____ *"What is your age? Race? Religion? Creed? Sex? Marital status?"*

_____ *"What is your best friend like?"*

_____ *"To what clubs or organizations do you belong?"*

_____ *"Who lives in your household?"*

_____ *"What is the name and occupation of your father/mother/spouse?"*

_____ *"What kind of military discharge do you have?"*

_____ *"Have your wages ever been attached or garnished?"*

Single

_____ *"Do you live alone? With someone? With your parents?"*

_____ *"How do you get along with your parents? Do you provide them with financial aid?"*

_____ *"Do you pay for room and board?"*

_____ *"Do you have a boyfriend/girlfriend? Is this relationship serious?"*

_____ *"What are your plans concerning marriage?"*

Engaged

_____ *"When do you plan to marry?"*

_____ *"What is the occupation of your future spouse?"*

_____ *"Do you plan to work after you are married? If so, how long?"*

Married

_____ *"What is your maiden name?"*

_____ *"Do you rent or own your home?"*

_____ *"What are your financial obligations?"*

_____ *"What is your spouse's occupation? For how long? Does he/she like that job?"*

_____ *"Is your spouse willing to have you work? For how long?"*

_____ *"Is there any possibility that you or your spouse will need to relocate?"*

_____ *"If both you and your spouse are working, for what will you use the extra money?"*

_____ *"What are your plans about raising a family?"*

Children

_____ *"Do you have children? If so, what are their ages? Their general health?"*

_____ *"Do you plan on having additional children?"*

_____ *"Who will be caring for your children while you work? At what cost?"*

_____ *"How will the school-age children be cared for during summer recess?"*

_____ *"How does your spouse feel about your leaving the children to go to work?"*

Divorced

_____ *"Are you divorced? Why? How long have you been divorced?"*

_____ *"What financial support do you provide to/receive from your former spouse?"*

_____ *"Who has custody of the children? Do you provide/receive support for them?"*

_____ *"Do you plan to marry again?"*

Arrest, Jail, and Conviction*

_____ *"Have you ever been arrested/convicted for a misdemeanor?"*

_____ *"Have you ever been arrested for other than a minor traffic violation?"*

_____ *"Have you ever been arrested and jailed for a felony?"*

(The only legal question is "Have you ever been convicted of a felony?")

"DO YOU HAVE ANY QUESTIONS?"

One of the last interview questions an employer may ask is *"Do you have any questions?"* The employer asks this as a common courtesy, and as one more test. The job-seeker who has no questions will not do well in this test. The employer will probably assume that this person has no serious interest in the position.

You will do well simply by having one or two questions ready. These questions should not be aggressive. Don't ask about salary and benefits. (Deal with these issues only after you are offered the job.) Your questions should be assertive and show concern for the position and the company. Rather than asking what the company can do for you, ask what you can do for the company.

The following list may serve as a guide to the kind of questions you might ask at the end of an interview. You may use questions from this list or make up your own. Don't waste your questions. Ask for information that really will be useful.

"What kind of training might I expect if hired for this position?"

"Is there anything I can do or study to get a head start on learning this job?"

"How much supervision would I receive as a new employee?"

"What hours will I be working if hired?"

"Will there be a chance to work overtime in this position?"

"May I see the area where I would be working?"

"What company is your biggest competitor?"

"What weakness do you find in my background, relative to this job?"

"Would you describe your own concept of the ideal employer?"

"How can I take on more responsibility here?"

Write the questions you want to ask an employer on three-by-five index cards. Take these and a JIST Card to the interview. You may not need to look at them during the interview. However, it is better to do so than to forget an important question or statement.

The Call-back Closing

Seldom will you be offered the position you want at the end of an interview. An employer will need some time to consider you for the position. The employer may have other applicants scheduled for interviews. You may be the best applicant so far. Still the employer must check other options if the position need not be filled immediately.

Usually an interview will end with the employer saying, *"I'll be contacting you soon to let you know my decision."* This should be your cue to begin your *call-back closing*. This closing arranges for you to contact the employer. You might say, *"I have several interviews scheduled, but I am very interested in this position. Rather than risk missing your call, when may I call you?"* The employer will appreciate this expression of your interest. Also, your call-back closing suggests that you should be hired soon — before another employer offers you a job.

At the end of the interview ask for the date and time to call back. Write this data down after you leave. Thank the employer for his or her time. Then present your JIST Card. You may say, *"Here is the number where I can be contacted if you need to reach me before I call."*

This kind of call-back closing is simple, yet powerful. In the last minute of the interview you will be asserting your interest, your value, and (with your JIST Card) your skills, abilities, experience, and good qualities! Then, when you call back as scheduled, you will be able to show once more that you are reliable and punctual.

Follow Up!

When the interview is over, don't just go home and wait for the phone to ring. Send a thank-you note that very same day. If you are genuinely interested in the job, say so in your note. Enclose another JIST Card, or at least provide your phone number again. Remember — the interviewer has spent his or her valuable time talking to you. For this alone, the interviewer deserves a thank you.

Handwritten notes are acceptable if your writing is neat and legible. Use good quality notepaper. Consider buying professional-looking thank-you notes at a stationery store in an ivory or off-white color. A clean, typed, professional-looking thank-you note is acceptable in all situations, and especially effective in formal situations. Following is a sample thank-you note that should help you write your own personal notes.

July 30, 1988

Dear Mrs. Rhoades:

Thank you so much for the time you spent with me yesterday. I know you were busy, yet you went out of your way to make me feel relaxed and comfortable during the interview.

The more I thought about the position we discussed, the more interested I became. I will be in touch with you soon to answer the questions you asked. In the meantime, I just wanted to let you know how much I appreciate the reception you gave me. It's no wonder you have so little turnover in your staff.

Sincerely,

Sandra Kijek

Sandra Kijek

"SORRY, WE CAN'T USE YOU JUST NOW."

When you call back, you may learn that another applicant got the job. You should not be discouraged if you are not offered a job. The time and effort you put into any interview will not be wasted.

Your interviewing skills will improve each time you put them to the test. You should become aware of weaknesses in your presentation as you use it. You can correct the weaknesses by figuring out how you can better meet an employer's expectations in this area. Practice makes perfect, and actual interviews make perfect practice.

The average job-seeker will just quit when the employer calls to say, *"Sorry, we can't use you just now."* However, you already know that you still have options when told there are no openings. You can use this moment to restate your interest and arrange another phone call, ask about other available positions, or get some job leads.

THE JOB OFFER

The more interviews you have, the more likely it is that you will be offered a job. Most job-seekers accept the first offer immediately. There are some things you should consider before accepting. Consider the position, the company, and the employer. Also consider other workers, salary, working conditions, benefits, shift and duties.

Consider if the separate elements of employment with a particular company seem satisfactory. The employer who offers you a position must value you. He or she should be willing to give you a reasonable amount of time to think over your decision (twenty-four hours at least). The employer should also be willing to answer further questions you may have. (**After** getting the job offer, you should ask about salary.)

You have options. You may accept the job on the spot, take time to think about it, or decline the offer and continue your job-search. Remember that a job-search is **not** successful just because it leads to a job. **The best measure of success is whether or not the job is one you really want and can do well!**

FINDING JOB LEADS

... uncovering the hidden jobs

Through your own dedicated work in this book, you have learned many ways to convince employers of your value to them. This new knowledge will serve you well. Such knowledge alone will not, however, insure your success. You also need lots of leads about job openings. The more leads you have, the greater your chances of finding the job you want.

How do you look for job leads? List below as many ways of finding job leads as you can think of. Try to think of at least five ways. Then circle those methods that you believe will be the most productive.

1. _____
2. _____
3. _____
4. _____
5. _____

6. _____
7. _____
8. _____
9. _____
10. _____

Job leads can be either **visible** or **hidden.** The visible leads are openings advertised in such places as newspaper want-ads and employment agencies. These visible leads are easy to find, and most job-seekers limit their job-search to pursuing these leads.

The hidden job leads are those openings that are never advertised. Because they are not listed in either the newspapers or with employment agencies, it takes some work to uncover these leads.

There are several reasons why you should not confine your job-search to the visible leads only, as so many job-seekers do. Many of these jobs offer little pay. Others demand special skills, which you are unlikely to have. Visible jobs also create lots of competition because so many job-seekers know about them.

The following statements show some of the attitudes job-seekers often have after pursuing visible leads. Perhaps you have heard these or similar comments. Perhaps you have even made them yourself.

"I have been looking for work these past six months now. What a total waste of time!"

"The employment office doesn't seem to be of much help. There are so many other people down there, anyway."

"I read the want-ads every day, but there are few jobs listed that I want. When I do apply, there are usually lots of people interested in the same job."

These statements show the false belief that very few job openings exist. And this brings us to the main reason why you should not limit your job-search to visible openings: **only 25 percent of all available jobs are ever made visible.**[1] This means that even the active job-seeker who depends on visible sources would be aware of only one out of every four job openings.

Jobs do exist. Even in the worst economic times, people retire, move, and quit. For these and other reasons, people are always being hired. In a slow economy, about 1 percent of the work force begins, leaves, or changes jobs each month. In more prosperous economic times, when jobs are easier to find, as many as 2 to 3 percent of all working people are in a job transition each month. In the U.S. this means that there are from one million to three million job openings each month.[2]

This chapter explores methods for finding job leads in both the hidden and the visible job markets. It then helps you use these methods to develop and follow up on your leads. As you read about these methods, compare them with the methods you listed at the beginning of the chapter. You will probably decide that you can make some big improvements in your list.

FINDING HIDDEN JOB LEADS

There are two very good reasons why you should concentrate on the hidden openings during your job-search. These two reasons are that

- most openings are hidden rather than visible, and
- there is less competition for the hidden openings.

For these reasons you are more likely to find the job you want and can do well in the hidden job market.

Contrary to what the name seems to imply, there are few mysteries about the hidden job market. Each hidden job has an employer with certain expectations about the right person for the job. The job is hidden merely because the employer chose not to list it in the newspaper or with an employment agency.

There are several reasons why employers decide not to make positions visible. They may decide that advertising a job is not worth the money, time, and effort required. They may not want to take time to deal with the countless applicants who are looking for "just any job." Employers may intend to fill a position with someone already employed by the company. Or,

---

[1]United States Department of Labor, Manpower Administration, *Career Threshholds*, Vol. 1, Manpower Research Monograph No. 16.

[2]Richard Lathrop, *Who's Hiring Who*, (Berkeley, CA: Ten Speed Press, 1980 revision), p. 19.

employers may sort through applications that are already on file. From these they can arrange interviews with the most promising applicants. Employers can even wait for the first good job-seeker who calls or comes through the front door.

Whatever the employer's reason, you need to solve the mystery *"How do I find hidden jobs?"* Once you find and apply the solution, your job-search will be ready for success.

Look at the chart titled *How People Find Jobs.* The data in this chart comes from the largest survey on the question of how people actually find jobs. When deciding what job-search techniques to use, it makes sense to choose those that worked well for others. Notice that the two most effective techniques listed in the chart are **applying directly to an employer** and **asking friends and relatives.** Let's look at how you can use these two methods to find hidden job leads.

How People Find Jobs

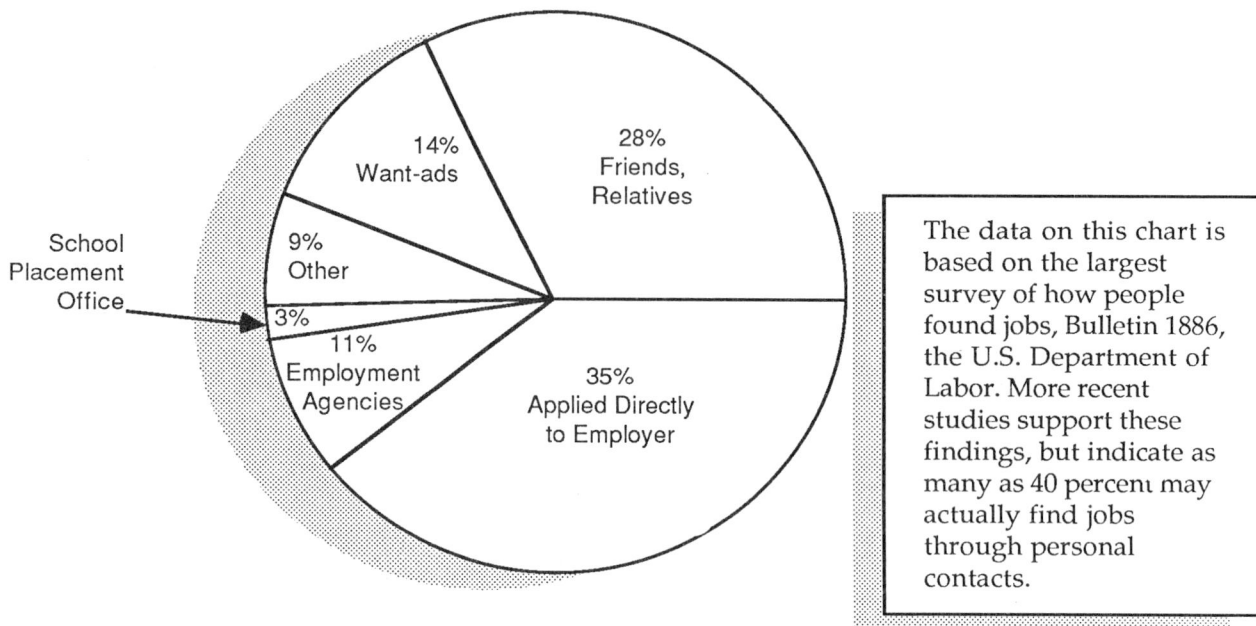

School Placement Office

14% Want-ads

28% Friends, Relatives

9% Other

3%

11% Employment Agencies

35% Applied Directly to Employer

The data on this chart is based on the largest survey of how people found jobs, Bulletin 1886, the U.S. Department of Labor. More recent studies support these findings, but indicate as many as 40 percent may actually find jobs through personal contacts.

Making Direct Contact with Employers

The most effective method of finding hidden jobs is to apply directly to the employer. Notice in the *How People Find Jobs* chart that more than one-third of all people who find jobs find their jobs using this technique.

Most job-seekers assume that there must be a job opening before they can obtain an interview with a prospective employer. This is not the case, however. Employers are willing to speak to job-seekers, even when no job opening exists. Smart employers know that they may need a good employee at some future time. Perhaps someone will quit, business may expand, or someone now on the job may be having problems.

Another factor is that some jobs are hidden from the employers! Many employers can create new positions as they see fit. An employer might do this if you prove you have skills needed by the company. So, in this case, the employer sees the right person, then sees the right job. For this reason, you should always be ready for a job lead to become an interview.

The first step in applying directly to employers is to make a list of prospects. This list should include all of the employers who might possibly hire you to do the job you want.

Your list of prospects should include the names, addresses, and phone numbers of businesses that might have the job you want. Further research can provide other useful data, such as the names of the people to whom you should speak. You can use several resources to make your lists. Following are brief summaries of the major resources you can use in developing a list of prospects for finding hidden job openings.

The Yellow Pages

The Yellow Pages of the phone book make an excellent resource for developing a list of prospects. The Yellow Pages have the most basic, current information about potential employers. In the Yellow Pages businesses are grouped by the kinds of products and services they provide. This means that you can easily compile a list of companies that might need your special skills. The Yellow Page listings will have the name, address, and telephone number of each company. Using your presentation you can turn this data into job leads and interviews.

Be complete and creative in your Yellow Pages research. Read all the headings from A to Z. List any that even slightly suggest the job you want. For example, if you wanted a job in food preparation you might first think only of restaurants. However, looking at the headings in the Yellow Pages you would see the following groups of jobs, and others, that might provide good leads for someone with a background in food preparation.

Sample Yellow Page Categories

Airline Companies

Airports

Amusement Places

Bakers, Retail

Banquet Rooms

Banquet Caterers

Banquets, Restaurants

Barbeque

Basket, Dinners,
   see Chicken Dinners

Beach, Motels,
   see Motels & Hotels

Beach, Resorts,
   See Resorts

Boarding Homes
   see Nursing Homes
   see Rest Homes
   see Sanitariums

Boat, Launching Sites

Bowling Alleys

Buffet Dinners,
   see Caterers

Bus Lines

Note that only the Yellow Page listings beginning with A and B have been listed. Food-service listings from C to Z have yet to be explored. And these are just the categories. Each category includes many potential employers.

Because there are so many potential sources of employment listed in the Yellow Pages, even in the phone directories of mid-size cities, it is important to determine whom you will contact and how. To make the best use of your time, you want to contact first the employers who are most likely to hire you. Therefore, for every category listed in the Yellow Pages, ask yourself, *"Could this kind of organization possibly use a person with my skills?"* If the answer is *"Yes,"* or even *"Maybe,"* list that category.

Some of the categories will sound more interesting to you than others. As you list a category, rate each one by writing "1" next to it if the category sounds very interesting, "2" if it sounds somewhat interesting, and "3" if it is not at all interesting to you. Following is a brief example of how someone looking for a position in food service might organize his or her prospect list from the Yellow Pages.

Yellow Pages Prospect List	
Types of Organizations	**Level of Interest**
Airline food companies	2
Airport cafeterias	2
Bakers, retail	3
Bakers, wholesale	3
Banquet caterers	1
Banquet restaurants	1
Beach resorts	1

After you have listed and rated the categories in which you might find a job, you need to list individual employers within each category. You will contact each employer listed under each category in the Yellow Pages. You may want to begin contacting employers you've rated "3." This will give you an opportunity to improve your skills in making direct contacts, while talking to the employers who have the jobs in which you are least interested.

Associations and Local Organizations

An *association* consists of a group of people with a common interest or purpose. Associations differ greatly in their makeup and function. All, however, are potential sources of job leads. In scope an association can be local, state, regional, or national. People who do similar kinds of work often form associations. A few of these associations are listed below. In the list below many of the associations are referred to as *State/Regional*. These associations would be listed in your area under the name of your state, city, or region. An example would be the *Chicago Hotel and Motel Association*.

American Road and Transport Builders Association

Associated Builders and Contractors

State/Regional Hotel and Motel Association

Home Builders Association

Association of Plumbing, Heating, and Cooling Contractors

State/Regional Association of Realtors

State/Regional Electronic Service Association

Federation of Licensed Practical Nurses

State/Regional Manufacturer's Association

State/Regional Food Processors' Association

National Motor Carriers

Labor Relation Association

State/Regional Restaurant Association

State/Regional Retail Council

State/Regional Service Station Dealers Association

Mechanical Contractors

National Association of Social Workers

National Retail Hardware Association

State/Regional Watchmakers Association

Society of Broadcast Engineers

Use the phone book to determine what associations are available and of use to you. Research the directory listings *Associations, Business Organizations, Trade Organizations,* and *Labor Organizations.*

When you contact an association, ask for a list of all the local businesses employing people to do the type of work you want. Also ask for any other information that might help you in your job-search.

You may want to join associations that you contact. This could help you get some inside information. By attending meetings you will get to know members of the association. These people may be able to help you in your job-search.

Some local organizations are socially or community oriented. These organizations may help you contact employers. You can find such organizations in the Yellow pages under *Associations, Community, Foundations,* and *Social-Service Organizations.*

The Chamber of Commerce

The *Chamber of Commerce* is an association. Its purpose is to improve business in a certain community. Your local Chamber of Commerce can be a good source of information on companies that might need someone with your skills. Many Chambers of Commerce, especially at the state level, publish directories. These directories contain data on area businesses. Thus, the Chamber of Commerce is not just a source for job leads. It is also a potential resource for research. Learning such things as a company's size and specialities will help you when an employer asks, *"Why do you want to work for us?"*

You can locate the Chamber of Commerce by checking the phone book. At the same time you might locate similar associations. Some examples are the business and trade organizations, and the community, state, federal, and social service organizations. The more you know about a company, the more confident you can be during an interview. However, having just the *name* of a company that needs someone with your skills is a good start. You can return to the phone book for the basic data you need to establish contact.

The Public Library

The public library is another valuable resource for hidden job leads. It is overlooked by many job-seekers. The library has countless materials to help you in your job-search. Just a few of these materials are described below.

- **Telephone Directories** — Many libraries have current phone books for the large cities. If you want a job in an area far from your home, these books will be very helpful. Even the local directories can be helpful if you want to avoid distractions at home or you do not have a phone book.

- **Newspapers** — The public library keeps the local newspapers on file. Many libraries also keep major out-of-town newspapers. The library's newspapers can be especially useful when you want to do research to prepare for an interview.

- **Business Directories** — Business directories have the names, addresses, and phone numbers of businesses and their managers. These directories also have other useful data. Some examples of such directories are *Poor's Register of Corporations, Directors, and Executives; The Thomas Register of American Manufacturers; Dun and Bradstreet's Million Dollar Directory; The Federal Register;* and the *Directory of Corporate Affiliations.*

- **Professional and Trade Journals** — Many professions and trades have their own journals and magazines. These publications are concerned with the current trends, history, and the future of their fields. They are outstanding resources. They can help you present an up-to-date, professional image in an interview. These journals may also have information about new markets in the profession or trade. And new markets mean new job leads!

Remember — the resources just mentioned are only a few of the many that you can find at the library. Keep in mind two other factors. First, the librarians can help you find the materials that you need. Second, the service your library provides is **free**.

Other Resources for Leads to Hidden Jobs

Other resources you develop for finding hidden job leads depend on your own insight and effort. Your research with the Yellow Pages, Chamber of Commerce, library, organizations, and family and friends should direct you toward countless resources. Each new resource may reveal still more leads.

Another helpful resource is the employment contractor specializing in temporary help. This person contracts to do short-term services for businesses, then hires people to do the job. The temporary job can last from one day to one year. This sort of work can help you make some "survival money" so you can continue your job-search.

Temporary work can also be a good source of useful information and job leads. If the temporary work is similar to your desired position, you can learn or review procedures and equipment operation. You can also pick up other information that will be important to your future job. Another advantage to temporary work is that you will probably be working with permanent employees. Many of these people can provide job leads. These people are likely to know of other places that are involved with similar products or services.

Temporary-help agencies hire people for the following types of jobs. Locate these agencies in the Yellow Pages under *Employment Contractors-Temporary Help*.

Types of Temporary Help			
Secretarial	Demonstration	Word Processing	Clerical
Unskilled Labor	Marketing	Data Processing	Security
Skilled Labor	Factory	Project Service	Maintenance
Technical	Assembly	Warehouse	

Remember — the more job leads you develop in the hidden job market, the sooner you will make direct contact with your next employer. Do **not**, however, put off contacting employers until you have completed your list of prospects. Your list and your research will probably never be completed! Contact your prospects as soon as you find out about them. You can continue your research for job leads in between contacts and interviews. In fact, you will get many job leads during your quest for interviews. You will learn to go about making direct contact with employers later in this chapter.

Friends, Relatives, and Acquaintances

Friends, relatives, and acquaintances are often overlooked by job-seekers as the important sources of job leads that they are. In fact, they may be your *best* source of hidden job leads. The *How People Find Jobs* chart shows that 28 percent of all people find their jobs from leads given to them by friends or relatives. Some studies found that when acquaintances are added to this category, the percentage rises to nearly 40 percent.

All of your friends, relatives, and acquaintances are sources of job leads. These people work in places where jobs open up and they know other people with job openings. Your goal is to let them know you are looking for a job. They can be especially helpful if they know what sort of job you are looking for and why you are qualified for that kind of job. One effective way to do this is to provide them with a JIST Card and discuss what you are looking for. Perhaps they know of a job opening in your field. If not, ask for the name of someone who might know of an opening.

Making Your List of Prospects

You probably know or have something in common with many more people than you realize. In the box below list all of the groups of people with whom you have something in common. Two of the most important groups have already been listed for you. If you are having trouble thinking of groups, the list below may give you some ideas.

```
┌─────────────────────────────────────────────────────────────────┐
│                    Groups of Prospects                            │
│                                                                   │
│   1. friends                        8. _____       │
│                                                                   │
│   2. relatives                      9. _____       │
│                                                                   │
│   3. _____          10. _____       │
│                                                                   │
│   4. _____          11. _____       │
│                                                                   │
│   5. _____          12. _____       │
│                                                                   │
│   6. _____          13. _____       │
│                                                                   │
│   7. _____          14. _____       │
└─────────────────────────────────────────────────────────────────┘
```

```
┌─────────────────────────────────────────────────────────────────┐
│                  Some Ideas for the Box above                     │
│                                                                   │
│   Neighbors                        People I socialize with        │
│                                                                   │
│   People who attend my church      People who provide services    │
│                                      to me (insurance agent,       │
│   People I went to school with       hairdresser, grocer, etc.)    │
│     (even grade school)                                           │
│                                    Friends of my parents          │
│   Former teachers, former employers                               │
│                                    Members of my social           │
│   People I used to work with         organizations                │
└─────────────────────────────────────────────────────────────────┘
```

After you've listed all of the groups with which you have something in common, you will need to develop a list of names from each group. As an example, let's look at the "friends" group. We'll say that a friend is anyone with whom you are reasonably friendly and who does not fit into one of the other groups you've listed. If you try your best, how many names could you think of for this group? Ten? Twenty-five? More?

On a separate sheet of paper write *"Friends."* On this sheet of paper list all of your friends. Each one of these people is a source of job leads. You should contact each person during your job-search.

Follow this same procedure with each of the groups you listed in the box above. How many names can you list for each group? Most people can think of well over one hundred names. And all of them can help you find out about unadvertised, "hidden" jobs.

Networking

A network is a group of people you know who do not necessarily know each other. Any person you know or come to know in your job-search can introduce you to others. The illustration at the top of the next page shows how you can begin job-search networks.

Two Job-Search Networks

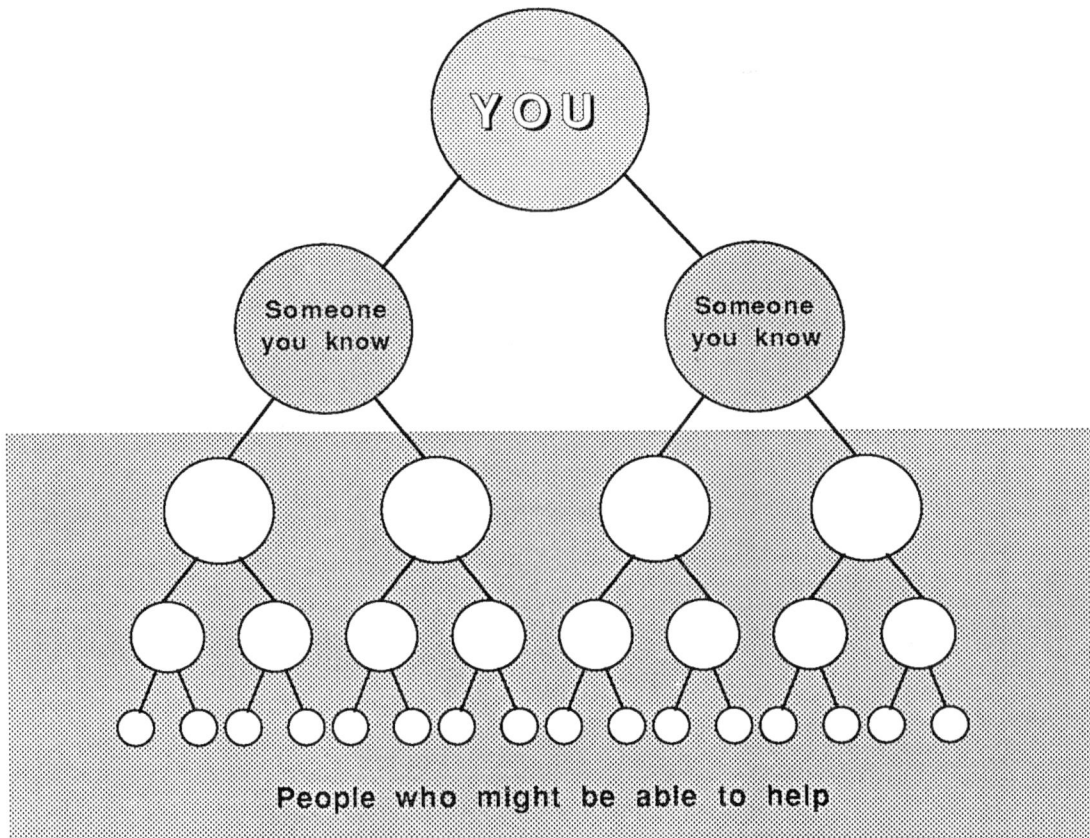

Suppose you ask your friend for the names of two people who might help you. You could contact these people, who would then become part of your job-search network. If each of these people gives you the names of two others to contact, and so on, you would eventually have many people in your network. And all from just one original contact!

Networking

Networking is *not* a job-search technique that you will use only with friends. You can start a network with any person — friend, relative, acquaintance — anyone. Work at building up more and more job-search networks as you use all of the different ways to find a job.

FINDING VISIBLE JOB LEADS

The visible job market includes only the jobs that are advertised, posted, or otherwise made available to the public. These jobs make up just 25 percent of all the actual job openings. Newspaper want-ads, employment and placement agencies, and government offices are the most common sources of these job leads.

Although you may be quite familiar with these traditional sources, you should carefully review them before using them in your present job-search.

Want-Ads

About 50 percent of all job-seekers use the newspaper want-ads as a source of job leads. Unfortunately only about 14 percent of all jobs are obtained through these ads.[1] Still, you should use the want-ads. They are the third-leading source of job leads in terms of jobs obtained. The trick is to use want-ads as just one part of your job-hunt and to use them to your best advantage. To appreciate the advantages of using want-ads, you should first review the disadvantages.

Disadvantages

Only 25 percent of all job openings are made public. The majority of these jobs appear in the newspaper want-ads. This mean that you will miss **at least** 75 percent of all job openings by relying on want-ads alone.

Competition can be fierce. When unemployment is high, over 10 percent of the total population looks at the newspaper want-ads every week. Half of these people are seriously looking for a job. This means that in a city of one million people, a hundred thousand people are reading the want-ads. If the newspaper has one thousand want-ads per day, there is only one job for every one-hundred job-seekers. Of course the odds are worse for the most desirable jobs. The bottom line is that a job-seeker depending only on want-ads is competing with anyone who can read!

Some employers use want-ads to create or expand their files of potential employees. However, few people are ever hired from these files. A survey of employers in two major U.S. cities showed that 75 to 80 percent of employers do not hire employees through want-ads. The other employers hire only one out of every twenty-four applicants who respond to want-ads.[2]

In many cases job openings are filled before the want-ads appear in the paper. These jobs go to the job-seekers who pursue hidden job leads. These job-seekers find the jobs while they are still hidden. Job-seekers who rely totally on the newspaper do not apply for jobs until the newspaper tells them to.

Many ads are for undesirable jobs (low pay, poor location). Many others are for jobs requiring unique skills. Ads are also placed for jobs with no future. These are jobs that a company needs done for only a short time.

Tips for Using Want-Ads

Despite the disadvantages, the newspaper want-ads can be helpful. Remember — about 14 percent of all jobs are obtained through want-ads. Limit the amount of time you spend using the want-ads in your job-search. Since only 25 percent of all jobs are advertised, spend 25 percent of your job-search time using the want-ads.

The Sunday and Wednesday papers tend to have more want-ads than other daily issues. Few employers are available on Sunday. Therefore, you will not lose valuable job-search time if you read the Sunday want-ads.

Read the entire *Help Wanted* section. Sometimes interesting jobs are listed in the least-expected place. For example, a secretarial position may be listed under *Administrative Assistant* or *Clerical Help*. If you only look under *S*, for secretary, you will not see the listing.

Mark all the interesting want-ads with a pen. Then write notes next to the ads if you have any questions or comments about the ads. Do this before you respond to the ads.

Pay attention to the type of employers hiring people with your skills. This will help you develop more leads. For example, a baker may find an ad placed by a hospital for a baker's assistant. The baker can assume that other hospitals have openings for bakers from time to time. Hospitals can then be added to the list of prospects.

If possible, research the company and person in charge of hiring before you respond to an ad. However, do not let the ad go unanswered for several days.

---

[1]United States Department of Labor, Bureau of Labor Statistics, *Job-Seeking Methods Used by American Workers*, Bulletin 1886.

[2]Olympus Research Corporation, San Francisco, *Feasibility Study Regarding Classified Ads in Daily Newspapers.*

If possible, research the company and person in charge of hiring before you respond to an ad. However, do not let the ad go unanswered for several days.

Want-ads may be in sections other than *Help Wanted.* Newspapers usually have information about new and expanding businesses. Such information can represent job leads. For this reason you should scan the entire newspaper.

Professional and Trade Journals

If you have a trade or profession, you may obtain publications that deal with your field. These magazines and journals publish information of common interest to people in your field. These publications sometimes publish want-ads. However, these ads lead to less than 1 percent of all jobs obtained.

Personal Ads

You can place an ad in the *Positions Wanted* section of a newspaper, trade magazine, or professional journal. This ad should describe the position you want, your skills, and how you may be contacted. However, you must weigh the cost of the ad against the results. Less than 1 percent of all jobs are obtained through these ads.

Employment and Placement Agencies

Most job-seekers use an employment agency or placement program in their job-search, but only 15 percent actually find a job with this method. Following are the percentages of job-seekers who have been successful with the various kinds of agencies and programs.[1]

Private employment agencies	5.6%
State employment security divisions	5.1%
School placement centers	3%
Other (unions, miscellaneous)	2%

This information shows that these agencies are not nearly as helpful as friends and relatives in obtaining jobs. There are times, however, when using agencies makes sense. Therefore, it is important that you understand what they can and cannot do for you.

Private Employment Agencies

Private employment agencies are in business to make a profit. They charge either the job-seeker or the employer, or both, for their services. Some of the problems with using these agencies are listed below.

- Less than 6 percent of all job-seekers obtain jobs through private agencies.

- Most agencies depend on a rapid turnover. These agencies do not usually spend much time helping any one job-seeker.

- Employers generate most of an agency's repeat business. This means that the agency's emphasis is on helping the employer rather than the job-seeker.

- Many agencies concentrate on filling entry-level job openings, which are easy to find. Other agencies specialize in professional and technical openings.

---

[1] United States Department of Labor, Bureau of Labor Statistics, *Job-Seeking Methods Used By American Workers,* Bulletin 1886.

- Only one out of every twenty people using a private agency gets a job through the agency. That's a 95 percent failure rate!

- Agencies charge fees ranging from 7 to 15 percent of the job-seeker's first-year pay. This could mean that you would pay well over $1,000 for a job you probably could have found yourself.

In some cases you should consider using a private agency. The following are a few such cases:

- When you yourself cannot spend much time on your job-search (when you are employed, for example).

- When you are willing to pay someone else to do something *The Work Book* can teach you to do yourself.

- When you have special, highly desirable, and sought-after job skills.

- When you accept only those referrals that include employer-paid fees.

State Employment Services

The United States Employment Service has programs to help people find jobs in every state. There are no fees for using these services. Most cities and many towns have a state employment office. The offices have different names in different states. Some common names include phrases such as *Employment Security* and *Job Service*. For an address, look in the Yellow Pages under the name of your state. These services are often called "unemployment" offices by people who use them.

You should go to the closest state office and register for work. Do not make this your only source of job leads, however. Read the following reasons why.

- Only about 5 percent of all job-seekers get their jobs through state services.

- In most cases the state offices know of only 5 percent of the available jobs.

- Since over one-third of all job-seekers register, competition is fierce.

- For a variety of reasons, many of the placements made by state services are not successful. Nearly 60 percent of the job-seekers leave these jobs within thirty days.

The best reason to use a state employment service is that it is free. It is also a very good source of training and vocational-testing information.

If you use a state agency, visit the office regularly. Try to see the same counselor each time. To get help, you must be persistent and patient! If you see the same counselor each time, the counselor will probably become more and more interested in helping you.

School Placement Centers

Jobs secured through school placement centers represent about 3 percent of all the jobs found. While 3 percent may not sound like much, school placement services have a very high success rate — for those who are fortunate enough to be able to use the school placement services.

It would be unwise for you to wait at home for the school placement office to call you for an interview, but you should take advantage of their services whenever possible. Stay in touch with the placement staff and do anything reasonable that they ask of you. Consider sending thank-you notes to the placement staff. They probably deserve the thank you, and you can always use more friends.

Government Employment

Federal, state, provincial, and local governments hire huge numbers of people — as many as one out of every five people hired. For this reason, you should definitely find out what government jobs you might qualify for and how to apply for them. Most phone books have a separate section in the White Pages for government services. Look through this section for the most likely departments. Call them, ask questions, and follow up as required.

You should realize that most government jobs require applicants to take civil service tests or to follow complex application procedures. All of this takes time. While you can often get an appointment to talk directly to the person who can hire you, this person often is forced to hire someone else. Hiring decisions are frequently regulated and based on test scores, application dates, and other factors. If you need a job quickly, do not rely completely on finding government employment.

Other Agencies

There are many agencies other than those mentioned that can help you find a job. Most of these concentrate on helping certain types of people. Most do not charge fees. If you qualify for their services, these agencies can be excellent sources of job leads and other information. Some of the people who qualify for the services of these agencies are listed below.

- **Job-seekers under the age of twenty-one** — Some public schools provide classes, job listings, and other help for job-seekers under the age of twenty-one. Many local, state, and federal youth programs are designed to help young people find jobs. Some of these programs concentrate on summer job placements.

- **Economically disadvantaged** — Many programs are available to people whose family incomes are lower than average. You may not consider yourself poor. However, you may still qualify for these programs.

- **Persons with physical or medical limitations** — Most regions of the country have programs to help people with handicaps find jobs. An example of such a program is the Bureau of Vocational Rehabilitation.

- **Women** — Many organizations have been very active in providing women with job-seeking programs. The YWCA is one example of such an organization.

- **Persons with other special needs** — There are still other programs available for job-seekers with special backgrounds or needs. Examples include job-seekers over fifty-five (senior citizens), armed-forces veterans, people with criminal records, immigrants, and clergy.

You may qualify for some special services. The Yellow Pages are a good place to start looking for agencies that can help you. If you do not know where to look, ask the telephone operator for assistance. After you find some leads, call the agencies. Ask what they have to offer and whether or not you qualify.

One warning — do not expect any agency to get you a job! An agency may provide you with job leads but it will also take time away from your own job-search.

HOW TO CONTACT EMPLOYERS

As soon as you begin to develop lists of potential employers, you should begin to make direct contact with those employers. How do you make direct contact? There are five basic ways:

- Personal referral
- Telephone contact
- Information interview
- Personnel office
- Resume campaign

The first three techniques are recommended for your own job-search. The other two are listed because they are common approaches. They are, however, less effective for most job-seekers.

Personal Referrals

The most effective technique for contacting employers is to have people the employers know and trust refer you to them. For example, suppose a friend of yours knows an employer who might have an opening in your area. You could contact the employer and introduce yourself as a friend of "John Jones," who, you would say, suggested that you contact the employer. When the employers know that you have been referred by a friend of theirs, they are usually very willing to help you. A personal referral is almost always the most effective way to make contact with a potential employer.

Telephone Contacts

The telephone will probably be your most effective tool in making direct contact with employers. Chapter 5 describes the whys and hows of using the phone. The telephone is time-efficient and cost-efficient. Even more important, it lets you talk with the employer person-to-person on first contact.

Using your telephone presentation and your list of prospects, call each company or organization in which you are interested. Ask to speak to the person in charge of the job you want. Then get that interview! With this method you will be directly contacting the person who can do you the most good. You will avoid those three or four levels of people who cannot help you very much.

Make as many calls as you can each day. Remember that your goal is to get interviews. If a contact does not lead to an interview, ask for more leads.

You may be thinking, *"Why can't I use the phone to follow up on the openings I already know exist?"* Well, you can! Using the phone is an easy way to follow up on want-ads and other visible job leads. Just be sure to speak with the person who can hire you.

The Information Interview

The *information interview* is another method for making direct contact with employers. You can use this method without ever applying for the job. You can also use information interviews to discover hidden job leads and gather valuable information.

To use the information interview, first contact a potential employer. Introduce yourself and express a sincere interest in the kind of work the employer manages. Then ask for an appointment to discuss the matter further. At that time you can interview the employer to find out about certain jobs and the business in general. You can also learn the names of other employers who can provide similar information.

The information interview can reward you in many different ways. Therefore, you should study the mechanics of the information interview in detail. Consider using this method in your own job-search.

Begin by identifying a few employers who manage jobs such as you desire. You can use any of your resources to locate these employers. Your research should produce at least the names, addresses, and phone numbers of a few businesses.

Next, you should contact an employer. Introduce yourself and explain your interest politely and briefly. Be enthusiastic! Read the following example.

"Hello, Mr. Tedrow. My name is Katherine Winters. I'm calling you because I am interested in the local printing and publications trade, and I am considering a future career in this field. I would be most interested in learning your personal views on it as an industry and as a career. I would very much appreciate your scheduling some time this week to share some of your insight with me."

Notice here that it is not obvious that you are looking for a job. Of course you are, and it is not honest to say that you simply want to collect information if you really want to be considered for future openings. Therefore, be prepared to explain that you are looking for a job and that you realize there are probably no openings in their organization at this time. You might say that you would still like an appointment because you are new to the field or because you want to know more about this kind of work from an expert such as the employer you are calling on.

When arranging your information interviews, be courteous, interested, and ready to meet the employer expectations. Do not even suggest that you are looking for a job. How will you ask for this interview? Write your presentation in the space below.

_____

_____

_____

_____

_____

Your goal is an information interview. This interview should be separate from your first contact with the employer. However, you should be prepared to conduct the interview during the first contact. If you choose to make your first contact with a personal visit, the employer may want to speak with you then. When you use the phone, some employers may refuse your request for a personal interview. They may, however, offer to answer a few questions over the phone. If you are prepared, just one minute of the employer's time can mean valuable information for you. It can even result in more job leads!

To conduct a successful information interview, you should be ready to meet the employer expectations. Your appearance should be the same as for a job interview. You will show your regard for attendance and punctuality by attending the interview on time. For this reason, make sure you write accurate notes when arranging the interview. You can emphasize the third employer expectation — skills — by referring to your skills as you ask questions.

When you go to the interview, you must be ready to ask several meaningful questions. Much of the success of your interview depends on the careful planning and writing of your questions. The employer will be more at ease if you are well prepared. The following questions are some examples of questions you might ask an employer during an information interview.

Information Interview Questions

"How did you first become interested in this business?"

"What do you most like/dislike about your profession?"

"What are the important areas for future development in this industry?"

"What are some typical daily pressures of managing this sort of business?"

"What personal qualities are necessary to succeed in this kind of business?"

"Would you recommend this profession to a person considering it for a career?"

"What can a person do to get a head start in learning to be a (job title)?"

"Would it be possible to arrange a tour of the facilities?"

"Do you think it reasonable of me to be considering a career in this profession? Besides my sincere interest in this specific area, I . . . (insert a major portion of your complete skills statement)."

"So far, in researching this profession, it seems to me that the right person for the job of, say, (title of position desired), should: (1) basically, look and act like a (title of position desired), (2) be punctual, reliable and dependable, and (3) have the skills, abilities, and experience necessary to perform well in this position. As an employer yourself, what do you think of this assessment? What other qualities might you recommend?"

"Do new employees in the (department of the desired position) generally receive on-the-job-training or formal training?"

"Would you agree that (your own good qualities from JIST Card) are the qualities of good workers in this trade?"

After you write your questions, pick the five to ten questions that you think will produce the most valuable information. You might write your questions out, leaving enough blank space between questions for notes. You should take notes during your interview. It is better to take notes than to forget something important. Also, your organization and interest may impress the interviewer.

Make some neat copies of your final list of questions. Then you will not have to make a new list for each interview. It should be fairly simple to revise your list later according to previous notes. Remember — the better your questions, the more relaxed and rewarding your interviews will be.

The Final Questions

The final questions on your list should be arranged as in the following example.

"I would like to learn more about this business. Can you recommend anyone else for me to contact?"

(Name _____. Company _____.

Other data about person or company _____.)

"May I use you as a reference when I contact this person?" (_____ yes _____ no)

These final questions will produce more leads. They will also get you onto another level in a network to direct contacts with employers. As you know, if you get the names of two people to contact from an interview, these names can lead to many additional contacts. With these contacts you will hear about openings before they are listed in the want-ads.

Keep It Short and Say, "Thank You"

Be sure to leave the interviews after thirty to forty-five minutes unless the employers ask you to stay. At the beginning of the interviews, tell the employers that you know they are busy. Tell them that you appreciate their time and will only stay thirty minutes or so. Do not stay over sixty minutes unless they insist.

Always be sure to thank the employers for their time. It is a good idea to send a thank-you note to each employer a few days later. This note will serve as a courteous reminder of your visit. The note will also supply the employer with your name, address, and phone number. You may include a JIST Card with the note. Having this information and knowledge of your interest, an employer may contact you when a job is available.

The Personnel Office

Most people think they should start their job-search in a personnel office. However, if you simply walk into a personnel office, you are not likely to talk with the person who can hire you. The personnel staff does not hire anyone. These people just screen and refer people for interviews. People on the personnel staff do not know of jobs about to open. They cannot create new jobs for exceptional people like yourself. This means that unless a job opening is listed, you will probably not be given an application in personnel. Instead, you will hear *"Don't call us, we'll call you."*

While personnel offices often do not hire workers, you can sometimes get some help from people in the personnel office. Check to see if any positions you might be interested in are posted. It's always possible. Go out of your way to get to know the people working in the personnel offices at a company in which you are particularly interested. Send these people notes, thanking them for the help they've given you. If a job becomes available, they are likely to remember someone such as you who has stayed in touch.

The Resume Campaign

Many job-seekers send out lots of resumes in the hope that someone will call them for an interview. While this technique does work sometimes, it is far more likely that you will waste your stamps. One study[1] indicated that a job-seeker would need to mail 245 resumes to "To Whom It May Concern" to get **one** interview. One lesson to be learned from this is that if you send out unasked-for resumes, be sure to address your cover letter to a person at that company — do not send your resume to "To Whom It May Concern" or to "Dear Sir or Madam." Better yet, call the person first and then send the resume (if you can't get an interview). And follow up! You'll learn how to prepare your resume in the next chapter.

---

[1]Deutsch, Shea, & Evans, Inc., *Electronic Design 16*, p. 173.

A Few More Job-Search Tips

Here are just a couple of pointers to keep in mind as you contact employers directly.

Small Businesses

Most traditional job-search techniques assume that you are looking for a job with a large business or organization. Yet most people work for small businesses. Small businesses are also a major source of all new jobs, and they often offer the best opportunities for learning and advancement. The pay and fringe benefits offered by small businesses frequently do not compare with those offered by larger companies, but a small business could be the place for you if

- you are just starting a new career,
- you are changing careers,
- you want more responsibility,
- you need a job quickly.

Many smaller organizations do not have a personnel office at all. This is good news since it makes the boss easier to contact. Just ask to see him or her — it is often that easy.

Always Follow Up

People who follow up get jobs. Send thank-you notes. Arrange to recontact on a regular basis people who appear to be either helpful or potential employers. Consider sending one or more JIST Cards and resumes both before an interview and after. Whatever follow-up actions you take will help people remember who you are and what you are looking for. You will also impress them with how well organized you are — and every employer wants an organized worker.

Dropping In

A very effective way to uncover leads is to simply "drop in" on employers. You can do this informally, and it is surprising how many people will be willing to see you. This is particularly true of smaller organizations. Be on the lookout for any organization that might be able to use a person with your skills. Drop in and ask to see the person in charge. If that person is busy, ask what would be a good time for you to come back.

USING ALL THE METHODS

You should now see that all job-search methods have disadvantages. To have the most effective job-search you must use several different methods. You must use your time wisely. This means spending more time with those methods that have worked well for other job-seekers. The chart on page 114 shows how effective the different methods are.

Sixty-five percent of all job-seekers spend only five hours a week looking for work. If you spend more time, you can expect to find a job sooner. You should be willing to spend as many hours looking for a job as you expect to spend working at it once you find it. For example, if you plan to work forty hours a week, spend forty a week on your job-search. If you spend only twenty-five hours per week, your job-search will take much longer.

You must decide how much time you will spend each week using each job-search method. In making your decisions, keep in mind how effective the methods are.

On the following worksheet a job-seeker has planned to use a variety of methods. The job-seeker has written a percentage-of-success rate next to each method. From these percentages the job-seeker figures how many hours per week to spend with each method. This job-seeker plans to spend thirty-four hours per week job-hunting. Multiplying thirty-four times the percentage of success gives the number of hours for each method.

Sample Worksheet for Job-Search Planning

Technique	Predicted % success		Total hours/week available		Hours/week to use this technique (rounded)
1. Apply directly to employer	35%	x	34	=	12
2. Ask friends and relatives	28%	x	34	=	9
3. Answer news ads	14%	x	34	=	5
4. Use state employment service	5%	x	34	=	2
5. Send out resumes	5%	x	34	=	1
6. School placement office	3%	x	34	=	1
7. Information interviewing	3%	x	34	=	1
8. Miscellaneous	7%	x	34	=	2

Notice that this job-seeker plans to spend most of his or her time using the most effective methods. Unless you have a good reason, do not spend more time using a job-search method than its success rate justifies. To determine how much time you should spend using each job-search method, fill out the worksheet below. Read the directions for filling out the worksheet.

1. Review the methods for obtaining job leads described in this chapter. Then list those that you plan to use at least part of the time. The most effective are already listed on the worksheet since you will probably want to use these.

2. Enter the percentage of success that you estimate for each method.

3. Enter the total number of hours per week that you plan to spend on your job-search for each method.

4. For each method, multiply the percentage of success times the total number of hours. This will give you the number of hours per week that you should use that method.

Job-Search Planning Worksheet

Technique	Predicted % success		Total hours/week available		Hours/week to use this technique (rounded)
1) Apply directly to employer	35%	×	_____	=	_____
2) Ask friends and relatives	28%	×	_____	=	_____
3) Answer news ads	14%	×	_____	=	_____
4) (other)	_____	×	_____	=	_____
5) (other)	_____	×	_____	=	_____
6) (other)	_____	×	_____	=	_____
7) (other)	_____	×	_____	=	_____
8) (other)	_____	×	_____	=	_____
9) (other)	_____	×	_____	=	_____
10) (other)	_____	×	_____	=	_____

SORRY, WE'RE NOT HIRING, BUT GOSH!... COULD YOU SHOW ME HOW TO WRITE A "KNOCK-OUT" RESUME LIKE THIS?... I'M LOOKING FOR A NEW JOB, MYSELF!

8

RESUMES

make your rez′-o͞o-mā′ pay

In preparing for your job-search, you have learned to make and use various paper tools. Now, after your *DataTrakt*, applications, and JIST Cards, you should consider making your own resume.

A resume does not get you a job. Unfortunately many people do not realize this. Most often the resume is the only tool they make. They write their resumes and have hundreds of them printed. They mail the resumes to potential employers. Then they wait for a flood of job offers. Generally they get back only a trickle of responses. The responses are usually form letters stating only that the resume has been received. Some responses contain, once in a great while, an invitation for an interview. Seldom is a job offered in response to a resume.

The resume can, however, serve a purpose. It is another tool that can be useful in drawing an employer's attention to **you.** Like a JIST Card, your resume will tell an employer who you are, how to contact you, and the position that you want. Your resume will also describe your experience, skills, and abilities. Your resume will be more detailed and formal than your JIST Card, however.

Your *DataTrakt* and JIST Card will help you make your resume. Refer to them as you work through this chapter. If you did not make either a *DataTrakt* or JIST Cards, be warned that you will waste time and effort. Your resume will **not** be complete without the organized information contained on your *DataTrakt* and JIST Cards.

Perhaps you think that you do not need a resume. Depending on the job you want, this may be true. However, many employers expect them. After completing this chapter, you can meet the employer expectations with a superior resume.

Remember what employers expect of job-seekers. Your resume will satisfy these expectations in the following ways.

- **Appearance** — Many employers expect to see your resume during your interview. If you have a resume, you can meet this expectation. Since all your paper tools will be neat and well organized, your resume will show good appearance. The effort and care that goes into your resume will demonstrate how you will perform on the job.

131

- **Dependability** — If you have a resume when an employer asks for it, you will be showing that you are dependable. Your resume will be better than most resumes that the employer will read. Your resume will imply your dependability since it will present a totally positive view of who you are and what you have to offer.

- **Skill** — Your *basic* resume will describe your skills, abilities, experience, education, and training. You may choose to make a *superior* resume, which would include specific duties, accomplishments, and responsibilities from your job history. A superior resume would also define and qualify your skill in a way that would emphasize your worth as an employee. In this chapter you will learn to make and use both basic and superior resumes.

You can write your resume in either of two basic forms. The most familiar form is the *chronological*. The other form is the *functional*. You should understand each form before you decide which is best for you.

THE CHRONOLOGICAL RESUME

The chronological resume form is the form people have traditionally used when making resumes. The chronological resume lists jobs and experiences in the order in which they occurred. Usually the present or most recent items are listed first. Then the next most recent item is listed, and so on.

Read the example of a simple chronological resume to the right. You can learn some of the basic principles involved in resume writing by looking at the example. Note how the items in the *Education* and *Experience* sections go "backward in time." Also note that the example is a reduction. An actual resume is 8½ by 11 inches in size.

The example resume is clear and correct. Gene Taylor has taken the time to prepare a good copy. There are no errors in spelling or grammar. Gene has carefully proofread his resume. The resume will make a positive impression on an employer.

Gene has clearly and completely listed the ways in which he can be contacted. This is a basic part of any successful resume. Gene has included his address. He has also listed both his work and home phone numbers. As a result he can be reached by either phone or mail.

GENE TAYLOR
123 Main Street
Littleville, Indiana 46209

(317) 555-1492 (work)
(317) 555-1980 (home)

EDUCATION:

1967-1971	Ball State University; Muncie, Indiana; B.S. Degree, Major: Accounting.
1963-1967	Littleville High School; Littleville, Indiana; Diploma

EXPERIENCE:

1975-Present	Sales Representative, Banko Company; Littleville, Indiana.
1971-1975:	Assistant Accountant, Banko Company; Littleville, Indiana
1970-1971:	Student Assistant, Accounting Department, School of Business, Ball State University; Muncie, Indiana.

PERSONAL:

Active in community affairs, willing to relocate.

References available upon request.

Gene Taylor has wisely omitted some data that many job-seekers include on resumes. Gene did not list his age, weight, health, or marital status. This type of information serves no real purpose on a resume and should not be included.

Although he indicated that his references are available, Gene did not write them on the resume. This is a courtesy to the people who will provide references for Gene. In this way no one will be bothered needlessly for information. Gene will provide a list of references after the employer shows definite interest — probably toward the end of an interview. This is also a courtesy to Gene himself. Gene knows that his references are more likely to recommend him enthusiastically if they are not contacted repeatedly.

In the basic resume form on the next page, write your own resume.

By putting your own information into the basic resume form, you have the makings of your first resume. If you think this resume is good enough for your desired job, transfer your information to an 8½ by 11 sheet of unlined paper. Your resume should be **typewritten** at least. Having it typeset on bonded paper is even better, although this is more expensive. Transfer your information and the section headings *Education, Experience,* and *Personal.* Omit the words *name, address, phone, job,* etc. Also omit the answer lines contained in the form. Refer to Gene Taylor's typewritten resume as a model.

After you have neatly typed your resume, be sure to check the spelling and grammar. Then make plenty of copies. You can do this yourself or have it done by a quick-print shop. Make sure the copies are **neat.**

Standard white paper will work. However, as you learned in Chapter 4, a white paper tool will blend in with all the other paper tools. To make your resume noticeably different, you should consider a colored paper. You should choose a color that permits easy reading, while being attractive and businesslike. Some recommended colors are beige, buff, cream, and pastel shades of yellow, tan, and blue. You could project a very professional image by having your resume match or complement the color of your JIST Card. You can find colored typing paper at most office, art and stationery supply stores. If you have your resume quick-printed or typeset, the printer should have the color of paper that you want.

If you use a basic resume, your resume will be similar to the resumes of most job-seekers. Depending on the kind of job you want, this may serve you well. If you will be using a basic resume, go to *Using Your Resume* in this chapter to learn how to use your resume during your job-search.

Do not delay your job-search to improve your resume. Use your other paper tools and your basic resume now. If you choose to do so, you can improve your basic resume while it is working for you.

BASIC RESUME WORKSHEET

Name _____ Phone _____

Address _____ Phone _____

_____ (List your home number.
If it will not be answered
during the day, also list
another number that will
be answered.)

EDUCATION

From _____ To _____ School _____

Degree _____ Location _____

From _____ To _____ School _____

Degree _____ Location _____

EXPERIENCE (List most recent job first and work backward through your history.)

From _____ To _____ Job Title(s) _____

Company Name _____

Location (city) _____ (state) _____

From _____ To _____ Job Title(s) _____

Company Name _____

Location (city) _____ (state) _____

From _____ To _____ Job Title(s) _____

Company Name _____

Location (city) _____ (state) _____

PERSONAL

_____

SUPERIOR RESUMES

Gene Taylor has written a good, basic resume. However, it can be improved. Following are ten rules for a *superior* resume. As you review these rules, see how many Gene followed. Put an *x* in the box beside each rule that Gene did **not** follow.

☐ 1. State career objective near the beginning of the resume.

☐ 2. Explain specific duties for each position listed.

☐ 3. Include individual accomplishments from each position.

☐ 4. Detail responsibilities from each position.

☐ 5. Make your resume brief but complete, with correct spelling and proper grammar.

☐ 6. Do not leave job gaps in the *Experience* section.

☐ 7. Make your resume neat.

☐ 8. Do not list salary requirements.

☐ 9. Do not include any negative statements.

☐ 10. Do not list references.

GENE TAYLOR   (317) 555-1492 (work)
123 Main Street   (317) 555-1980 (home)
Littleville, Indiana 46209

EDUCATION:

1967-1971	Ball State University; Muncie, Indiana; B.S. Degree, Major: Accounting
1963-1967	Littleville High School; Littleville, Indiana; Diploma

EXPERIENCE:

1975-Present	Sales Representative, Banko Company; Littleville, Indiana.
1971-1975:	Assistant Accountant, Banko Company; Littleville, Indiana.
1970-1971:	Student Assistant, Accounting Department, School of Business, Ball State University; Muncie, Indiana.

PERSONAL:

Active in community affairs, willing to relocate.

References available upon request.

You should have put an *x* in each of the first four boxes. Gene Taylor can make his resume outstanding by improving these areas.

He should list a career objective after his name, address, and phone number. He has a clear statement of the position desired on his JIST Card. His statement reads, *"Position Desired: Sales Representative."* This will be the basis for his career-objective statement on his resume. He can transfer the statement to his resume by writing "CAREER OBJECTIVE: *Position as a sales representative."*

Gene can still improve his career-objective statement. First, Gene should foresee the possibility that an employer does not hire sales representatives. Gene should be more general and say he wants a position *in sales.* Gene should also make his statement in terms that describe action. Some useful words and phrases can be found on pages 149, 150. Employers want an active employee who is eager to accept responsibility. Gene should state his desire for *"a challenging position"* or *"a responsible position."* This will set Gene apart from those applicants who only want *"a position."*

You can further improve your career-objective statement by adding some mention of your skills. Gene Taylor can do this. His resume shows that he began with the Banko Company as an accountant and later moved into sales. Doing this Gene learned how a sales operation works in relation to the complete company. He can indicate in his career-objective statement that he is looking for a position requiring this particular skill. His final career-objective statement could be "CAREER OBJECTIVE: *A challenging position in sales. Ideally, this position would involve interaction with other departments in the company."*

It is a fairly simple process to create your own career-objective statement. First you should write the title of the position you desire.

Career Objective: A position as a _____

Improve your basic career-objective statement by adding a word or phrase that implies action. Make sure the position you list is not too specific.

Career Objective: _____

The position you want should require one or more of your strongest skills. Complete this second part of your career-objective statement.

Ideally, this position would require _____

_____

Now write your complete career-objective statement.

My Career-Objective Statement

Career Objective: _____

_____

_____

_____

There are still three parts of Gene Taylor's resume that need improving:

- Explaining specific duties for each position
- Including individual accomplishments from each position
- Detailing responsibilities from each position

These three areas of concern all relate to the *Experience* section of the resume. It is obvious that more information is needed to improve this section.

By using the example form at the right, Gene can organize his information so that he can easily transfer it to his resume. Only one job is shown in the example. However, the form should be filled out for each position in the *Experience* section. Notice that Gene has used specific terms of measurement, such as *"doubled"* and *"increased . . . 32%,"* to show the value of his accomplishments. Think of some similar measures of your accomplishments.

Dates Held: *1975* — *Present* Position: *Salesman, Benko Co.*

Explanation of Position: *Salesmen at Benko are concerned with making direct-to-customer sales in customer's homes.*

Responsibilities of Position: *The promotion of the full line of home service products made by Benko. Sales in the rural areas of a two-state territory.*

Accomplishments in Position: *Sales in my territory doubled during the years I held the position. I suggested a modification of the accounting system which saved staff time and increased profits by 32%.*

Develop your statements about your duties, responsibilities, and accomplishments in previous positions. Write your statements in the forms provided. Begin with the present or most recent position and work backward. If you wish to list more than three positions, use a separate sheet of paper.

JOB 1

Dates Held: _____ — _____ Position: _____

Explanation of Position: _____

_____

Responsibilities of Position: _____

_____

_____

Accomplishments in Position: _____

_____

_____

JOB 2

Dates Held: _____ — _____ Position: _____

Explanation of Position: _____

_____

Responsibilities of Position: _____

_____

_____

Accomplishments in Position: _____

_____

_____

JOB 3

Dates Held: _____ — _____ Position: _____

Explanation of Position: _____

_____

Responsibilities of Position: _____

_____

_____

Accomplishments in Position: _____

_____

_____

You should now have a great deal of information to use in making a superior resume. Carefully review your information about previous jobs. Pick out those items that present your skills in the most positive way. Then use this information to rewrite your basic resume. The added information will help convince employers that you are more qualified than applicants who have submitted only basic resumes. If you have not had many jobs, include any volunteer, school, or other experiences that show your abilities. Describe the duties, responsibilities, and accomplishments involved in detail.

Now Gene Taylor can write a superior chronological resume by using the information from his form. See the example at the right. Gene decided that for the job he wanted, his experience was more important than his education. Therefore, he reversed the order of the *Experience* and *Education* sections. For the same reason he simplified the *Education* section. He did this by omitting his high school record and listing only his college degree in accounting. Thus, he includes the one feature of his education that will be of most interest to employers.

GENE TAYLOR   (317) 555-1492 (work)
123 Main Street   (317) 555-1980 (home)
Littleville, Indiana 46209

CAREER OBJECTIVE:

A challenging position in sales. Ideally, this position should require a knowledge of how the sales force of a company functions as part of the whole structure of the company.

EXPERIENCE:

1975-Present   Sales Representative, Banko Company; Littleville, IN

I was responsible for direct-to-customer sales in the rural area of a two-state territory. I promoted the 150 home service products and doubled sales in my territory. I also suggested a modification of the company's accounting system which resulted in sales efficiency and a 32% increase in company profits.

1971-1975:   Assistant Accountant, Banko Company, Littleville, IN

I was responsible for maintaining an accurate record of the sales activity of Banko's 75 sales representatives. I was able to revise the handling of incoming records to clarify the sum total of sales activity.

EDUCATION:

1967-1971   Ball State University, Muncie, IN
Bachelor of Science Degree, Major: Accounting.

PERSONAL:

Active in community affairs, willing to relocate.

References available upon request.

As you prepare your own superior resume, try to select the words that best express your goals and summarize your experiences. The worksheet that follows provides a general format for your resume. If you have more data than this form allows, work on a separate sheet of paper. See page 151 for an example of a superior chronological resume.

SUPERIOR CHRONOLOGICAL RESUME WORKSHEET

Name _____   Phone _____

Address _____   Phone _____

_____

CAREER OBJECTIVE

_____

_____

EXPERIENCE

From _____ To _____   Position _____   Company _____

Location (city) _____   (state) _____

Explanation _____

Responsibilities _____

Accomplishments _____

From _____ To _____   Position _____   Company _____

Location (city) _____   (state) _____

Explanation _____

Responsibilities _____

Accomplishments _____

From _____ To _____   Position _____   Company _____

Location (city) _____   (state) _____

Explanation _____

Responsibilities _____

Accomplishments _____

EDUCATION

From _____ To _____   School _____

Degree _____   Location _____

From _____ To _____   School _____

Degree _____   Location _____

PERSONAL _____

THE FUNCTIONAL RESUME

The *functional resume* focuses on your most important skills. It supports these skills with specific examples of how you have used them. The functional resume lets you emphasize those skills that you believe are most important. It is **not** a chronological listing of your job history. This means that it can help you hide a lack of experience and job gaps. See the end of this chapter for an example of a functional resume.

To prepare a functional resume you must know what your skills are. You must also know which of these skills you would like to use on your new job. Vocational assessment, career exploration, and interest-testing will help you determine the skills that your resume should emphasize. You should also use your *DataTrakt*, your JIST Card, and the Employer Expectation exercises in Chapters 1 and 2. Then make a list of your skills and examples of how you applied them. When thinking of examples, consider your entire job experience, education, and training.

In the example at the right Gene Taylor listed one of his skills. He then listed some ways in which he used that skill in previous jobs. Job titles, names of employers, and dates of employment are of **no** concern. The skill, its application, and the resulting accomplishments are the important items. Gene will use this same format to detail his other skills.

> Skill: **Organization**
>
> Applied in Job 1: **Modification of the accounting system to improve organizational efficiency.**
>
> Accomplishment: **Increased profits 32%, increased sales efficiency by 17%.**
>
> Applied in Job 2: **Revision of Record Handling**
>
> Accomplishment: **Clarification of Total Sales Activity.**

In the first blank below write a personal skill that you consider important to the position you want. If necessary, refer to your JIST Card. Then list the specific ways that you have applied this skill. Also list the accomplishments that resulted.

Skill: _____

Applied: _____

_____

Accomplishment: _____

_____

Applied: _____

_____

Accomplishment: _____

_____

If you make a functional resume, use the format above to detail **all** your skills. Be sure to look at the examples of functional resumes at the end of this chapter before you make your own resume.

USING YOUR RESUME

Your resume is a highly detailed paper tool. You will want to use it often in your job-search. Some of the uses of a resume are similar to those described for your JIST Card. For example, after filling out an application, attach your resume with a paper clip or staple. If you do this, potential employers are more likely to see you as you want them to see you.

As a Business Card

After an interview you may leave your resume with the interviewer as a "super" business card. Thank the interviewer for his or her time. Arrange for a follow-up phone call. Later your resume will remind the employer who you are and what you have to offer. The resume will also tell the interviewer how to contact you. Your resume will describe in detail how you meet all the employer expectations.

Information for Your References and Network Members

You may want to give copies of your resume to your references. The resumes will help these people write and speak positively about you. Your resume will supply your references with information about the position you currently want. With this information on your resume they can discuss how your experience and qualifications relate to the position you want. Your resume will also help remind former employers exactly when you were employed and what your position was.

Your references are people who have favorable opinions of you and your abilities. These people may know you only from one situation, such as work, school, or church. With a copy of your resume each person will be aware of your other experiences. This added information can help your references highlight your history.

Also give copies of your resume to family members and friends whom you have asked to "be on the lookout" for potential jobs. Your resume will remind them of the kind of position you want. When the opportunity comes up, your "lookout" can give a resume to a potential employer.

Publicizing You

Mail your resume to potential employers. However, do not mass mail your resumes randomly. Remember — if you mail 245 resumes randomly, you can expect to receive just one request for an interview. You will be far more successful if you use your resumes to follow up specific leads. After promising telephone contacts you can mail resumes to those certain employers. Perhaps a telephone contact almost, but not quite, got you an interview. A follow-up resume and another phone call might do the trick.

You can use your resume with your other paper tools to follow up job leads. This amounts to your own "media blitz." Say, for instance, you use the Yellow Pages to make a successful telephone contact. You are invited for an interview. You have prepared your paper tools and practiced interviewing. Therefore, you will be successful in filling out your application and handling the interview. At the end of the interview you will arrange for a follow-up phone call and present your JIST Card. When you make your follow-up call, you will express your increased interest and offer to send your resume. Your resume will remind the employer of who you are, what you have to offer, and how you can be contacted. You will have the employer's favorable attention. Your chances of getting the position will be **far greater** than those of the average job-seeker.

Cover Letters

You should **always** include a *cover letter* when you mail your resumes to potential employers. The cover letter is the first thing the employers should see and read. It introduces your resume.

Your cover letter should be brief and interesting to insure that your resume will be read. Here are some rules to follow in preparing your cover letter:

- Always send your cover letter to someone in particular. Do not send it to anyone in a personnel department unless you know the name of the person who supervises the position you want. Be certain that you have all names, titles, departments, and other details spelled correctly.

- Make your letter neat and error-free. As with your resume, appearance counts. One error or one case of poor physical appearance will create your first and last impression with that employer.

- Target your letter to the situation. A few typical reasons for sending a cover letter and resume include preparing an employer for your interview (the best reason), responding to an ad, and following up a phone call after you have promised to send information. Each situation requires a different approach. Take advantage of the opportunity to provide special information that is not on your resume but which may be of particular interest to the employer.

- Be clear about what you want. If you want an interview, ask for it. If you are very interested in the particular organization or position, say so, and then tell why you think you would do a good job. An informal and friendly, but professional, style that avoids the hard-sell ("Hire Me Now!") usually works best.

- Plan to follow up. Do not expect someone to contact you. Instead, mention that you will contact the person at a specific time unless an interview or some other activity is already set.

Following are sample cover letters, which have been written for some of the more common situations. Use these samples to build on and expand as you develop your own letters.

Informal Cover Letter
Sent Prior to Interview

```
                                          628 Holly Road
                                          Starlight, Pennsylvania 15339
                                          February 29, 1990


Ms. Mary Smith, Director of Operations
Short Optical Corporation
2020 Vision Way
Starlight, Pennsylvania  15339

Dear Ms. Smith:

When our mutual friend, Jane Logan, suggested that I call you, I had
little hope of getting through to you so quickly.  Thanks so much for
setting up an appointment to see me so soon.  I have been interested
in the vision business for some time now, and I believe I am ready to
make my contribution to this field.

Just seeing firsthand how an efficiently managed and growing organization
works will be a worthwhile experience for me.

I have enclosed my resume for your information.  I will be at your office
promptly at 9 a.m. next Thursday, March 5.

                          Sincerely,

                          Debbie Doring
                          Debbie Doring
```

5413 Harrison Avenue
South Bend, Florida 41267
September 5, 1989

Mr. Paul McLoughlin
The Travel Store
1900 Avenue of the Americas
New York, New York 10052

Dear Mr. McLoughlin:

As promised, I have enclosed a copy of my resume. Please look it over
within the next few days. Perhaps you will think of a few people whom
I can contact.

Your suggestions for breaking into the travel business in New York have
already been helpful. I called Ms. Kijek right after I spoke with you,
and she has agreed to see me during my trip to New York. Thank you
for the lead. She made me promise to say hello when I spoke with you
next.

Based on the good reception I have received, I have now made firm plans
to be in New York during the last week in October. I would like to
see you if at all possible during that week. I will call you soon to
arrange a meeting.

Thanks again for all of your support in my job-search. Please call
me at home if you hear of anyone who is looking for a bright and
ambitious (and willing to learn) travel agent.

                    Sincerely,

                    Fred Warren

                    Fred Warren

7221 W. Place
Stevensville, Kansas 62348
March 23, 1989

Mr. Bob Arnold, Personnel Director
Anonomous Corporation
223 Placer Drive
Stevensville, Kansas 62347

Dear Mr. Arnold:

I read with interest your ad for a secretary in the Stevensville Times.
As requested I have enclosed my resume for your review. Since I am
certain that you will receive lots of resumes, let me give you a few
reasons why you should sort mine into the "I want to interview this
person" pile.

I have selected the secretarial field as my career. For me, it is not
just a way to earn a living. As proof of this, I have taken a variety
of secretarial courses throughout high school and have completed the
Professional Secretarial Program at the Stevensville Business Institute.
This is a one-year, full-time program with course work in accounting,
office management, word processing, and other advanced topics. Besides
receiving a B-plus average in this tough and demanding program, I held
a full-time job at the same time.

In addition to my training, I have had a variety of work and life
experiences, which help me understand more than most people my age.
For example, I have learned to work quickly with large numbers of
customers in a busy restaurant environment. The sensitivity to people's
needs and ability to solve problems quickly are as useful in an office
as they are in other work settings.

Being dependable is also one of my virtues. I have not missed a day
of school or work, for example, during this past year. In fact, I like
to work. I like being with people, staying busy, and doing assignments
well.

Since you will probably need to make a decision on this soon, I will
give you a call this Friday morning, March 28, to provide answers to
any questions you may have. While I will be busy in my job search during
most week days, you can leave a message for me at any time on my
answering machine. I will return your call at my earliest opportunity.

                    Sincerely,

                    Robert Redfork

                    Robert Redfork

Points To Remember

Following are some tips and guidelines that will help you prepare and make use of your resume.

- Ask a friend or vocational counselor to read the first draft of your resume. Ask for suggestions on how to improve it.

- Always use action words, short sentences, and specific examples. You want *"a challenging position."* You are an *"experienced"* worker. You *"have dealt"* with a number of specific tasks.

- Make sure that everything in your resume relates to the position you want. Do not waste even one second of an employer's time with unrelated details.

- Do not limit the possible uses of your resume by listing a specific job title in your career-objective statement.

- Do not spend so much time writing your resume that your job-search is delayed. Follow the guidelines in this chapter. You should be able to complete a well-organized resume fairly soon. After using your resume, you can better determine which parts, if any, need improvement.

- At the least, have your resume neatly typed. For the best possible results, have it typeset and printed on good quality paper.

- Try to get your entire resume on one sheet of paper (8½ × 11). If you are typing your resume, use only one side of the paper. If you have your resume typeset, you may have it printed on the back as well as the front of the paper. An employer is more likely to read the entire resume if it appears to be short. You can get a lot of information on one side of one sheet of paper.

RESUME EXAMPLES

The following pages contain examples of actual resumes. There are both good and bad elements in each resume. There is no one right way to do a resume. The examples are here to give you ideas. Read each resume and evaluate it. Then read the critique of that particular resume on page 148. The critiques note a few of the good and bad points, but not all. You should now be able to point out other problems and successes on your own.

You will also find two more examples of different ways to present your resume on the final pages of this chapter. You can use these resumes, and all the others in this chapter, to obtain ideas for preparing your own, unique resume.

JOHN H. SHEADY

80 Harrison Avenue
Laurel, California 99643

Home: (303) 379-8276
Message: (303) 786-6780

JOB OBJECTIVE:

An effective and articulate problem solver, seeking a responsible position in a sales or service oriented organization.

AREAS OF EXPERTISE:

Communications:
Relate in a friendly, yet personal style with people of diverse backgrounds. Have considerable experience in formal and informal sales presentations to groups as large as 300 persons. Able to express self clearly in a variety of written formats including complex formal proposals, statistical summaries, correspondence and promotional pieces. A sincere interest in and desire to please others facilitates relaxed, one-to-one communications.

Sales:
Over a period of years, have consistently demonstrated superior achievement in representing products and services in many different settings. In the competitive food service industry, "converted" over $1,000,000 revenue annually from competing accounts. Had the highest sales of over seventy-five people in my division nationally. As an account representative with The Great Widget Company, personally handled sales contracts as large as $150,000. Not simple "order taking," these sales required complex, technical presentations; detailed report writing; considerable pre-sales planning; and group presentations. Required extensive travel over a fourteen state region.

People Skills:
Have ability to quickly gain trust and confidence. As customer sales representative for a major corporation, accumulated over eighty unsolicited complimentary letters from customers. In various positions in supervision and management have consistently demonstrated the ability to increase the morals and productivity of people at all levels. Have supervised staffs as large as 15 people.

Problem Solver/Analyzer:
Able to approach large and complex systems and resolve problems to maximize efficiency. In many cases, a product or service was involved as a tool in the problem resolution process. Successful implementation of the proposed improvements required the purchase of the service. Simply phrased, created a need for a previously unused service or product. One example involved the use of data processing techniques which resulted in a savings to one customer of over $200,000.

Persistence/Energy:
In virtually all tasks undertaken, have used a natural and spontaneous personal energy to perform beyond expectations. A desire to successfully complete projects provides the motivation to achieve excellence. Example: As sales representative, was assigned half the medical facilities in Illinois. During allotted time, visited ALL facilities in area — many of whom had not been visited in over three years. Made additional follow up visits to many of these facilities and *still* remained in the allotted time frame. Results were a 110% increase in annual sales from this region.

EDUCATION:

Northwest Community College — Computer Science/Math
Argyle Business College — Business Degree
One week or longer courses in: Sales, Supervision, Management, Customer Service, Public Speaking, and related topics.

PERSONAL:

Married seven years; enjoy challenges; active in community affairs; a participant rather than an observer in life.

REFERENCES AVAILABLE UPON REQUEST

JOHN H. SHEADY

80 Harrison Avenue
Laurel, California 99643

Home: (303) 379-8276
Message: (303) 786-6780

FRANK E. PERKINS

9272 Kessler Boulevard
Indianapolis, Indiana 46235
(317) 555-0119 or 555-9761

CAREER OBJECTIVE

Challenging purchasing position with progressive opportunities where proven talents and skills in . . .

Negotiation
Problem Solving
Supervision & Organization

. . . . . can be effectively utilized to our mutual benefit.

TYPICAL ACCOMPLISHMENTS

Throughout twenty years of work experience, a variety of skills and capabilities have been demonstrated. Among them:

COST ANALYSIS
— Analyzed cost data on $650,000 inventory.
— Purchased raw materials for processing in the area of $4,000,000 annually.

COST EFFECTIVENESS
— Interviewed vendors to obtain information on products, prices, quality, and delivery.
— Developed 200/300 new vendors, increased 300% competitive bidding, thereby realizing lower prices.
— Succeeded in getting vendors to go on a cost plus 10% basis.

SUPERVISION AND ORGANIZATION
— Supervised, directed, and trained 8-10 people in taking physical inventory.
— Designed inventory tags and four-part shop order ticket using NCR paper, saving company 750 hours annually as well as 30 reams copy paper.

POSITION HELD

1960 to 1980
— Service Supply Company, Indianapolis, Indiana
Buyer and Accountant

EDUCATION

— Indiana University, Major — Accounting

PERSONAL QUALITIES

— Ability to plan and make decisions rapidly. Independent, self-motivated, adaptable, and reliable.

LILI LI LU[1]
1536 Sierra Way
Piedmont, California 97435
Telephone 436-3874

OBJECTIVE

Program development, coordination, and administration

Especially in a people-oriented organization where there is a need to assure broad cooperation through the use of sound planning and strong administrative and persuasive skills to achieve community goals.

MAJOR AREAS OF EXPERIENCE AND ABILITY

Budgeting and management for sound program development

With partner, established a new association devoted to maximum personal development and self-realization for each of its members. Over a period of time, administered budget totaling $285,000. Jointly planned growth of group and related expenditures, investments, programs, and development of property holdings to realize current and long-term goals. As a result, holdings increased 25 fold over the period, reserves invested increased 1200%, and all major goals for members have been achieved. (A number have been sharply exceeded.)

Purchasing to assure smooth flow of needed supplies and services

Usually alone (but in strong give and take consultation with partner concerning major acquisitions), made most purchasing decisions to assure maximum production from available funds. Maintained continuous stock inventory to determine ongoing needs, selected suppliers, and assured proper disbursements to achieve a strong continuing line of credit while minimizing financing costs. Handled occasional "crash" needs so that no significant project was ever adversely affected by failure to mobilize necessary supplies, equipment, or services on time.

Personal development and motivation

From the beginning, developed resources to assure maximum progress in achieving potential for development among all members of our group. Frequently engaged in intensive personnel counseling to achieve this. Sparked new community programs to help accomplish such results. Although arrangements with my partner gave me no say in selecting new members (I took them as they came), the results produced by this effort are a source of strong and continuing satisfaction to me (see "specific results" below).

Transportation management

Jointly with partner determined transportation needs of our group and, in consultation with members, assured specific transportation equipment acquisitions over a broad range of types (including seagoing). Contracted for additional transportation when necessary. Assured maximum utilization of limited motor pool to meet often-conflicting requirements demanding arrival of the same vehicle at widely divergent points at the same moment. Negotiated resolution of such conflicts in the best interest of all concerned. In addition, arranged four major moves of all facilities, furnishings, and equipment to new locations — two across country.

Other functions performed

Duties periodically require my action in the following additional functions: crisis management, proposal preparation, political analysis, nutrition, recreation planning and administration, stock market operations, taxes, building and grounds maintenance, community organization, social affairs administration (including VIP entertaining), catering, landscaping (two awards for excellence), contract negotiations, teaching and more.

Some specific results

Above experience gained in 20 years devoted to family development and household management in partnership with my husband, Harvey Hwangchung Lu, who is equally responsible for results produced. Primary achievements: Son Lee, 19, honor student at Harvard majoring in physics, state forensics champion. Daughter Su, 18, leading candidate for the U.S. Olympic team in gymnastics, entering prelaw studies at the University of California, Berkeley, this fall, Son Kwan, 16, a senior at Piedmont High School with 3.98 average, president of the student council, organizer and leader of a highly successful rock band, but heavily disposed toward future studies in oceanography. Secondary achievements: A lovely home in Piedmont (social center for area teenagers). Vacation homes in Newport, Oregon (on the beach) and a cabin in Big Sur. President of Piedmont High School PTA two years. Organized a successful citizen protest to stop incursion of Oakland commercialism on Piedmont area. Appointed by Robert F. Kennedy as coordinator of his campaign in Oakland.

Personal data and other facts

Born in 1934. Often complimented on appearance. Bachelor of Arts (Asian History), Cody College, Cody, California. Highly active in community affairs. Have learned that there is a spark of genius in almost everyone, which, when nurtured, can flare into dramatic achievement.

---

[1]Adapted from **Who's Hiring Who?**, by Richard Lathrop, Ten Speed Press, 1977.

Critique of John Sheady's Resume

Under *Career Objective* John Sheady says that he wants a job in sales or service. After John chose this objective, he used the *Dictionary of Occupational Titles* (available in public libraries) to find out what skills are needed for that job. He then included these skills in his resume.

John personally circulated his resume among his friends, relatives, and acquaintances. He got the job lead for his new position through this method. John's new job paid $6,000 a year more than his previous job.

On the positive side, the language in John's resume is action oriented. The format is clean and interesting, the emphasis is on skills. This resume does not show that John was unemployed (although he was), or that he does not have a college degree (he does not). In fact, this resume does not offer any negative information.

On the negative side, employers do look for work experience. This resume does not include any since this would suggest that John has been "job-hopping." Minor faults include the statement *"references available on request"* and the double listing of his address. The statement is unnecessary, as is the second listing of address.

Critique of Frank E. Perkins' Resume

Frank Perkins has presented his experiences in the best possible way. No negative points have been noted in his resume. The format is clean and interesting. Frank used numbers to document the degree of his responsibilities and accomplishments. His sentences are short and his words are action oriented. Frank handles his lack of a college degree well by simply listing, at the end, that he **did** attend a major university.

Critique of Lili Li Lu's Resume

This is a functional resume. It has fairly long narrative sections. The form is not fancy, but it is still quite impressive. Lili Li Lu is obviously a competent and experienced person, capable of doing many different jobs.

Note how the personal data is handled. Lili Li Lu placed *Education* at the end of her resume. Since she has so much experience, her education is less important and should be at the end. Besides, a degree in Asian history has little to do with her job objective. The last line under *Personal data* reflects Lili's sense of personality. It is a good idea to include such statements when possible. If you have not guessed her occupation, Lili Li Lu is a homemaker.

USEFUL WORDS AND PHRASES

It is important to use action words and short sentences in a resume. Employers want to know what you accomplished in previous jobs, school, and volunteer work. This is no time to be shy! Look through the following list of words and phrases. Pick out those that fit you and apply to your desired job. See if you can use these and similar words in your own resume. Even if you have never worked, you have hundreds of skills and abilities. Check those that you have used in previous jobs and other activities. Also check those that would apply to you in a future job.

About You and Your Strengths

____enthusiastic	____a fast learner	____a problem-solver	____dynamic
____competent	____trustworthy	____a coordinator	____reliable
____organized	____talented	____a manager	____a specialist
____motivated	____a leader	____efficient	____skilled
____effective	____cooperative	____a trainer	____punctual
____responsible	____an administrator	____an achiever	____a troubleshooter
____assertive	____dedicated	____a willing worker	____bilingual
____a risk taker	____a generalist	____a developer	____a motivator

About Your Experience

____comprehensive	____intensive	____general	____extensive
____successful	____solid	____competent	____specific
____broad	____consistent record of (growth, promotion, progress, etc.)		

About Your Abilities and Skills

____plan	____develop	____assist	____reduce expenses
____conceive	____create	____communicate	____increase profits
____supervise	____delegate	____recruit	____establish priorities
____interview	____understand	____modify	____schedule
____solve problems	____implement	____analyze	____practice
____write, compose	____train, teach	____innovate	____initiate
____work well with others		____increase productivity	

Relating to Data

____synthesize	____coordinate	____analyze	____compare
____complete	____compute	____copy	

Relating to People

____mentor	____negotiate	____instruct	____serve
____supervise	____divert	____persuade	____help
____speak/signal	____communicate	____take instruction	____understand
____poise	____encourage others	____develop support	____crisis intervention
____public speaking	____team member	____accept supervision	____interpersonal skills
____persuasive	____hire/fire	____debating	____promote
____influential		____develop trust	

Relating to Things

____set up	____manage money	____selling	____design
____operate/control	____write reports	____sports	____produce
____organize	____policy making	____program development	____tending
____coordinate	____precision work	____summarize	____manipulate
____research	____driving/operating	____work well under pressure	____planning
____numerical ability	____handle	____comprehend	____purchase
____appraise	____evaluation	____artistic presentations	____filing/typing
____install	____memory skills	____initiate projects	____calculate
____demonstrate	____budget	____fund raising	____act
____perform music	____bookkeeping	____showmanship	____building

Now circle at least ten words or phrases in the preceding lists that best describe you and your qualifications. Of course, these should represent skills that you most want to use in your next position. Also, you should be able to give an example of how you have used each skill or ability. Then use these words in your resume. Write out examples that demonstrate how you used these skills. Make sure that these skills relate to your career-objective statement. You might as well get paid for doing those things that you can do well and enjoy doing.

For more information about resumes, check your local bookstores and libraries. If you need help in finding the books you need, ask the salesperson or librarian.

A Sample Chronological Resume

Judith J. Jones   (317) 653-9217 (home)
115 South Hawthorne Avenue   (317) 272-7608 (message)
Chicago, Illinois 46204

POSITION DESIRED

Seeking position requiring excellent management and secretarial skills in office environment. Position could require a variety of tasks including typing, word processing, accounting/bookkeeping functions, and customer contact.

EDUCATION AND TRAINING

Acme Business College, Indianapolis, Indiana. Completed one year program in Professional Secretarial and Office Management. Grades in top 30% of my class. Courses: word processing, accounting theory and systems, time management, basic supervision & others.

John Adams High School, South Bend, Indiana. Graduated with emphasis on business and secretarial courses. Won shorthand award.

Other: Continuing at my own expense (Business Communications, Customer Relations, Computer Applications, other courses).

EXPERIENCE

1981 to 1982 – Returned to Business School to update skills. Advanced coursework in accounting and office management. Learned to operate word processing equipment including Wang, IBM, DEC. Gained operating knowledge of computers.

1979 to 1981 – Claims Processor, Blue Spear Insurance Company, Indianapolis, Indiana. Handled 50 complex medical insurance claims per day – 18% above departmental average. Received two merit raises for performance.

1978 to 1979 – Assistant Manager, Judy's Boutique, Indianapolis. Managed sales, financial records, inventory, purchasing, correspondence & related tasks during owner's absence. Supervised four employees. Sales increased 15% during my tenure.

1976 to 1978 – Finance Specialist (E4), U.S. Army. Responsible for the systematic processing of 500 invoices per day from commercial vendors. Trained and supervised eight others. Devised internal system allowing 15% increase in invoices processed with a decrease in personnel.

1972 to 1976 – Various part time and summer jobs through high school. Learned to deal with customers, meet deadlines and other skills.

SPECIAL SKILLS AND ABILITIES

80 words per minute on electric typewriter, more on word processor; can operate most office equipment. Good math skills. Accept supervision, able to supervise others. Excellent attendance record.

PERSONAL

I have excellent references, learn quickly, and am willing to relocate.

A Functional Resume

Mary Hummel

806 West Indiana Avenue
Montgomery, Michigan 49768

(222) 187-6027
(222) 187-6949

-CAREER OBJECTIVE-

Seeking an accounting position utilizing energetic, responsible and quality-oriented individuals with a proven history of achievement.

COST CONTROL FISCAL MANAGEMENT

2 1/2 years responsibility, $100,000 per year retail outlet. Responsible for opening and closing, maintenance of inventory, insured proper charges for orders, made night deposits and documented. Quality monitoring of cash and records ensured smooth operations and continuation of small business.

3.85 grade point average (15 months) in areas of:
- Accounts Payable and Receivable
- Double Entry
- Inventory Control and Valuation
- End of Period Summary
- Cost Accounting
- Federal Tax

Proven success at academics reinforces potential worth as employee.

SOPHISTICATED BUSINESS EQUIPMENT OPERATION

Capable and enthusiastic operator of:
- Word processor (Wang, Lanier)
- Data Processor (IBM System 36)
- Electric and manual typewriters
- 10-key adding machine and electronic calculator

Became volunteer instructor for 10 individuals (3 months)
Trainees' achievements, during instruction, resulted in their successful completion at training element.

PLANNING ORGANIZATION

Primary responsibility of ensuring timely and accurate completion of long-range, team-approach accounting projects. Kept time line, and made contact with critical group members.
Solid planning shown by superior academic achievements of group members.
Inherent organizational behaviors seen by proven capacity to plan, organize, and manage academic, family, and work life activities.
Above average success in all areas.

INTERPERSONAL PERSONAL SKILLS, TRAITS

- Elected to office of Treasurer (FFA), Student Council, and co-chairperson of National Honor Society.

- Development of customer relationships in retail outlet manifests self through "0" customer complaints over 2-1/2 year time frame and 200 (approximately) person per week volume.

- Volunteered as tutor in areas of math and accounting. Those who received instruction had positive evaluation of instructor.

ACADEMIC ACHIEVEMENTS

- National Honor Society (2 years).
- Earned Distinguished Scholastic Accomplishment, Rotary and Exchange Clubs.
- Named Student of the Month.
- Kellogg Community College Board of Trustees Award for Academic Excellence.
- Named to Dean's List and Honor Roll.

EDUCATION

- Graduate of Argubright Business College, Battle Creek, Michigan. Major: Business Administration and Accounting.
- Graduate of Marshall High School, Marshall, Michigan.

-PERSONAL CHARACTERISTICS-

Strong work ethic, career focused. Accepts instruction and will pay my way through reliability, hard work, and loyalty.

WELL, HERE I GO. I *KNOW* WHAT TO DO; NOW I'VE JUST GOT TO *DO* IT!

WORLD OF WORK

ORGANIZING YOUR JOB SEARCH

... ready, set, go!

You now know a great deal about job-hunting. You will know much more than most of your competitors. *Knowing* something, however, is not the same as being good at it. As you have learned throughout this book, being good at job-hunting requires **practice.** And the best way to get job-hunting practice is to go out and do it!

It's Time to Get Started! You must now **use** what you know. The best possible practice comes from applying what you have learned to a real job-search. It was suggested earlier that you spend as many hours each week looking for a job as you expected to work once you found one. Spend as much time as possible on your job-search. Remember — even if you spend only twenty-five hours you will be spending many more hours than most other job-seekers.

What's the Worst Thing That Can Happen? As you begin to use some of the methods you have learned, you may feel uncomfortable, shy, and afraid of making mistakes. This is natural. You will sometimes be aware of what you could have done better. In school, work, and life, this process is called *learning.* **Do not** let this fear of making mistakes keep you from going on. Understand that one interview is just one of many you will have. There will be bad ones as well as good ones. There will be rude employers, just as there are rude people in all other positions. The trick is to learn from every experience you have during your search. Improve those things that can be improved, and **keep on going!**

This chapter contains some schedules and forms that will help you in your job-search.[1] These paper tools and their functions are listed below.

- **Sample of a Daily Job-Search Plan** — This sample presents a day in the life of a job-seeker. It outlines the necessary daily activities. The plan shows when to do the activities and how to do them. It also lists the materials that you will need. You can follow this sample plan or modify it to better suit your own needs.

- **Daily, Weekly, and Monthly Job-Search Planning Calendar** — These forms act as your "appointment book" during your job-search. You will not want to forget when and where your interviews are.

- **Networking and Direct Contact Forms** — These forms are based on several job-search ideas presented in Chapter 7.

- **Follow-Up Cards** — These are 3″ × 5″ cards designed to remind you of the details of each contact and how to follow up.

Do remember in using these forms and schedules that your objectives should be fairly simple:

- commit at least twenty-five hours per week to your job-search

- arrange two interviews per day

- do your best in interviews

- follow up

If you do these things, you will get a job faster than if you do not. It is that simple.

DAILY JOB-SEARCH PLAN

A Sample

8:00 A.M. Get Ready!

I. Equipment you will need
   A. A clean desk or table on which to work — Make sure you work in a quiet place where there are few distractions.
   B. A telephone — It should be one that you can use without a lot of interruptions.
   C. *The Work Book* — You need the book as a reference to keep your job-search skills sharp.
   D. The newspaper want-ads, the Yellow Pages, and other sources of new job leads.
   E. Pencils and pens, envelopes, stamps, 3″ × 5″ cards.

II. Forms you will need
   A. Completed Telephone-Contact Script
   B. JIST Cards
   C. Resumes (if you have/need them for your search)

III. Can you think of anything else?

---

[1]The publisher grants users permission to reproduce the forms in this chapter for personal use only — not for resale or other distribution.

8:30 A.M. Gather New Leads!

From all sources get at least fifteen new job leads. For each lead, prepare a follow-up contact card before you make any calls.

  I. Check your networking lists
    A. Are there any friends, relatives, or acquaintances whom you have not yet contacted?
    B. Have you prepared a follow-up contact card for each person?

  II. Check your direct contacts list
    A. What other types of organizations could you possibly contact today?
    B. Prepare follow-up contact cards for each organization selected.

  III. Other sources — Use any other source of job leads available, such as want-ads and employment agencies.

9:15 A.M. Check Your Old Leads

Check old follow-up cards, planning calendars, and other sources for people you can call back today.

9:45 A.M. Take a Break!

10:00 A.M. Make Telephone Contacts!

  I. Do you have these things?
    A. Telephone in front of you — Anything not used in telephone contact should be cleared away.
    B. Your Telephone-Contact Script in front of you — You can read from it until you have it memorized.
    C. Follow-up cards — Use these for the new leads you are going to call today.
    D. Other information — Use this to make call-backs and do other follow-ups.
    E. Planning calendar — Record new appointments for interviews and other activities.
    F. Pencil or pen and other supplies.

  II. Begin making your calls
    A. Call all new leads, make call-backs, and do other follow-ups that you planned for today.
    B. Do not make a call until you have recorded the results of your previous call on your follow-up cards and planning calendars.
    C. If necessary, send thank-you notes, resumes, and JIST Cards for any calls that you have just made.
    D. Plan to make enough calls to get two interviews a day. This should take from twenty to thirty calls. Getting one interview, your minimum goal, should take you ten to fifteen calls.

11:30 A.M. Wrap It Up!

  I. How many telephone contacts did you make today? to new leads? call-backs? calls to friends and relatives?

  II. How many interviews did you get today? What companies? Where? On what days? What times? Whom will you talk to? Is this information on your Planning Calendar?

  III. How many applications, JIST Cards, and resumes do you need to drop off, fill out, or mail? What companies? Where? On what days? What times? To whom? Is this information on your Planning Calendars?

  IV. What about call-backs? Do you have new ones to do tomorrow? Did you get any new leads from your calls to friends and relatives? Did you note this information on your follow-up cards?

12:00 NOON Pat yourself on the back and go to lunch!

1:00 P.M. Begin Your Active Job-Search

I. Go to your interview appointments.

II. Keep appointments to fill out applications, and drop off JIST Cards and resumes. Try to set up interviews when you visit companies.

III. Things to do if you do not have appointments.
   A. Visit companies for whom you would like to work. Try to set up interviews.
   B. Set up information interviews with "hard-to-crack" companies.
   C. Check in with any agencies or offices helping you with your job-search.
   D. If you have a vocational or job-placement counselor, check in with that person.
   E. Get more leads and make more phone calls.
   F. Work on thank-you notes for interviews you have had. Put together more JIST Cards. Finish your resume (if necessary). Complete any other work important to your job-search.
   G. Call or visit friends and relatives you have not yet told about your job-search. Check back to see if others have found out anything that could help you.

5:00 P.M. You Are Done For The Day! Good Job!

Looking for a job is hard work. Find the time to relax and enjoy yourself with your friends or family. Make the time to do something you enjoy as a reward for your hard work.

Even on your off time you can let people know you are looking for a job. Everyone is a possible contact for you and can become part of your network. You can also use evening and weekend time to read or review job-search materials, work on improving your resume, contact your working relatives, or do other job-search activities.

Use the sample plan you've just read to make up your own plan. Your plan may be shorter or longer on some days, but you should use the same basic ideas for your own daily schedule.

PREPARING YOUR OWN JOB-SEARCH SCHEDULES

In Chapter 7 you decided on the number of hours per week you planned to spend looking for a job. Now you need to break that number of hours into a daily schedule.

1. How many hours per week do you plan to spend looking for a job? Be honest with yourself. Write a number you can stick to: _____

2. Which days of the week do you want to spend looking for a job? Circle those days in the box below. (Remember there are no more than eight work hours in a day.)

Sunday	Monday	Tuesday	Wednesday	Thursday	Friday	Saturday

3. How many hours will you spend looking for a job on each of these days? In the box on the next page, write the number of hours next to the days you circled.

4. What time periods during these days do you want to spend looking for a job? On the second line next to the days you circled, write in the times you will be conducting your job-search. For example, you may want to work on your job-search from 8 a.m. to 5 p.m. If so, you would write "8 a.m. to 5 p.m." on the second line.

5. Put these days and times on your monthly job-search calendar (bottom of page 158) for each week of the month. You should do this at least four weeks in advance. Planning your schedule this far in advance will prevent you from scheduling less important events during these times.

Scheduling Worksheet

Days	Number of Hours	Time Periods
Monday	_____	_____ to _____
Tuesday	_____	_____ to _____
Wednesday	_____	_____ to _____
Thursday	_____	_____ to _____
Friday	_____	_____ to _____
Saturday	_____	_____ to _____
Sunday	_____	_____ to _____

Use one daily/weekly calendar (page 159) for each separate week of your search. As you make appointments for interviews and other activities, list the place and kind of appointment. List this information in the corresponding time block under the correct day. Use the monthly calendar to schedule the active job-search time you planned. Also list any interviews you schedule or future reminders.

Try to make your job-search a daily routine. If you follow a routine similar to the sample daily job-search plan earlier in this chapter, your calendar will be very important in keeping you organized.

Now use the calendars on pages 158 and 159 to organize each day, week, and month of your job-search. Remember — getting a job is a job in itself! It is helpful to organize your days into four-hour blocks of time. This is similar to a typical eight-hour working day. Work from 8 a.m. to noon gathering leads and making telephone contacts. After lunch work from 1 to 5 p.m. keeping interview appointments, visiting companies, and doing other activities.

NETWORKING FORMS AND CONTACT LISTS

In Chapter 7 you learned how to develop networks of people who can help you develop job leads. You also learned how to develop leads for making direct contact with employers. As your networks and lists of direct contacts grow, you will need to carefully organize and keep track of your leads.

One organizational tool you will need is a Networking Form. You will use this form to list the people and organizations you plan to contact for one day. Create a simple form of your own using the entries and headings in the sample form on page 160 to guide you.

A direct-contact list is another simple form you can make on your own sheets of paper. You will use this form to list the companies and organizations within the Yellow Page categories described in Chapter 7. At the bottom of page 159 is an example with sample headings and entries. Since you will not usually have much information about these contacts, you will postpone preparing a follow-up card until after you have finished the call.

FOLLOW-UP CARDS

If you follow the suggestions in this book, you can develop hundreds of contacts to use in your job-search. You will not be able to keep track of all of these leads unless you keep notes and develop a way to organize your information.

On page 160 you will find an example of a completed follow-up card that you can make yourself using 3″ × 5″ cards available at most office supply and drug stores. Prepare one card for each person or organization that you may want to follow up with later.

Get an inexpensive file box with tabbed dividers for your cards. You will need one divider for each day of the month. When you want to follow up with someone on, let's say, the 15th of the month, put that follow-up card behind the 15th. When that date comes up, you will know exactly whom to contact.

GOOD LUCK!

Good luck on your job search. Job-hunting is often discouraging, and it can be one of the most difficult jobs you ever have.

Take care of yourself and don't give up. If necessary, accept a "survival" job while you continue to look for the job you **really** want.

You now know the most effective job-search techniques. It's up to you to use them. Luck will play a part, but remember — the harder you work, the luckier you are likely to be.

Monthly Job-Search Calendar

SUNDAY	MONDAY	TUESDAY	WEDNESDAY	THURSDAY	FRIDAY	SATURDAY

Daily and Weekly Job-Search Calendar

	Sunday	Monday	Tuesday	Wednesday	Thursday	Friday	Saturday
8:00							
8:30							
9:00							
9:30							
10:00							
10:30							
11:00							
11:30							
12:00							
12:30							
1:00							
1:30							
2:00							
2:30							
3:00							
3:30							
4:00							
4:30							
5:00							
5:30							
6:00							
6:30							

Sample Direct-Contact List

Category: <u>Cafeterias</u>

Name of Organization	Address	Phone Number
1. Albert C. Smith's Eatery	8614 N. Central Avenue	782-5699
2. Alfonso's Cafeteria	29 North Way	467-2211
3. Brenda's Place	Southway Drive	779-8257
4. Fritz Farkel's	4513 Armstrong Drive	329-4068
5. Jonathan's Inn	Johnson Street	526-7782
6. Lisa's French Foods	86 Central Avenue	669-4415

Sample Network Form

Name	Organization/ Referral	Follow Up Prepared?	Comments
1. Mary Hines	Friend of John Pass	Yes	Knows people
2. Fred Farkel	Friend	yes	Following up
3. Speth's Bakery			I shop there
4. Silver Lake Bakery	Want ad	yes	Baker's position
5. Miller's Grocery	Want ad	yes	Baked Goods Department
6. Uncle Paul's Chinese Eatery	Listed in magazine	yes	Irish/Chinese Food
7.			
8.			

A Sample Follow-Up Card

Organization: Silver Lake Bakery

Contact Person: John Smith   Phone: 421-9987

Source of Lead: William Henry - former supervisor

Notes: Called 2/21/86; Mr. Smith is on business trip, will be back 3/2/86. Call then.

NOTES

CALL-BACK CLOSING STATEMENTS

1. _____

_____

_____

2. _____

_____

_____

3. _____

_____

_____

4. _____

_____

_____

5. _____

_____

_____

6. _____

_____

_____

7. _____

_____

_____

8. _____

_____

_____

9. _____

_____

_____

10. _____

_____

_____

11. _____

_____

_____

12. _____

_____

INTERVIEW CALL-BACK CLOSING STEPS

At the close of the interview, when the interviewer says, *"We'll call you,"* you will

1. Thank the interviewer by name while shaking hands good-bye.

2. Tell the interviewer that you want and can do the job . . . only if you can and do.

3. Ask for a specific time and date that you can call back and ask follow-up questions.

4. Give the interviewer your personal business card.

5. Thank the interviewer again and assure him or her that you will be calling on the agreed upon date and time.

6. **Send a thank-you note to the interviewer and the secretary.**

13. _____

_____

_____

14. _____

_____

_____

15. _____

_____

_____

16. _____

_____

_____

17. _____

_____

_____

18. _____

_____

_____

19. _____

_____

_____

20. _____

_____

_____

21. _____

_____

_____

22. _____

_____

_____

23. _____

_____

_____

24. _____

_____

_____

QUESTIONS TO ASK EMPLOYERS DURING INTERVIEWS

1. _____

_____

2. _____

_____

3. _____

_____

4. _____

_____

5. _____

_____

6. _____

_____

7. _____

_____

8. _____

_____

9. _____

_____

10. _____

_____

11. _____

_____

12. _____

_____

EMPLOYER REFERENCES

JOB 3

Employer Name (Last) _____ Phone _____

Employed From_____ to_____ Start Salary_____ End Salary_____

Last Position Held _____ Supervisor _____

Duties/Responsibilities _____

_____

_____

Work Quality _____ Work Quantity _____

Interpersonal Skills:

Co-Workers _____ Supervisors _____

Attendance _____ Punctuality _____ Company Loyalty _____

Willingness to Do Extra Work _____ Reason for Leaving _____

Most Valuable Characteristic _____

Least Valuable Characteristic _____

Given Opportunity, Would Consider Rehiring Y ☐ N ☐

   If no, why? _____

JOB 4

Employer Name (Last) _____ Phone _____

Employed From_____ to_____ Start Salary_____ End Salary_____

Last Position Held _____ Supervisor _____

Duties/Responsibilities _____

_____

_____

Work Quality _____ Work Quantity _____

Interpersonal Skills:

Co-Workers _____ Supervisors _____

Attendance _____ Punctuality _____ Company Loyalty _____

Willingness to Do Extra Work _____ Reason for Leaving _____

Most Valuable Characteristic _____

Least Valuable Characteristic _____

Given Opportunity, Would Consider Rehiring Y ☐ N ☐

   If no, why? _____

EMPLOYER REFERENCES

JOB 1

Employer Name (Last) _____ Phone _____

Employed From_____ to_____ Start Salary_____ End Salary_____

Last Position Held _____ Supervisor _____

Duties/Responsibilities _____

_____

_____

Work Quality _____ Work Quantity _____

Interpersonal Skills:

Co-Workers _____ Supervisors _____

Attendance _____ Punctuality _____ Company Loyalty _____

Willingness to Do Extra Work _____ Reason for Leaving _____

Most Valuable Characteristic _____

Least Valuable Characteristic _____

Given Opportunity, Would Consider Rehiring Y ☐ N ☐

    If no, why? _____

JOB 2

Employer Name (Last) _____ Phone _____

Employed From_____ to_____ Start Salary_____ End Salary_____

Last Position Held _____ Supervisor _____

Duties/Responsibilities _____

_____

_____

Work Quality _____ Work Quantity _____

Interpersonal Skills:

Co-Workers _____ Supervisors _____

Attendance _____ Punctuality _____ Company Loyalty _____

Willingness to Do Extra Work _____ Reason for Leaving _____

Most Valuable Characteristic _____

Least Valuable Characteristic _____

Given Opportunity, Would Consider Rehiring Y ☐ N ☐

    If no, why? _____

PERSONAL REFERENCES

Reference #1

Name _____

Address _____

City, State, ZIP _____

Phone (h) _____ Phone (w) _____

Time known _____ Relationship _____

Occupation _____ Company _____

Has: ☐ Resume ☐ Work History ☐ JIST Card

Reference #2

Name _____

Address _____

City, State, ZIP _____

Phone (h) _____ Phone (w) _____

Time known _____ Relationship _____

Occupation _____ Company _____

Has: ☐ Resume ☐ Work History ☐ JIST Card

Reference #3

Name _____

Address _____

City, State, ZIP _____

Phone (h) _____ Phone (w) _____

Time known _____ Relationship _____

Occupation _____ Company _____

Has: ☐ Resume ☐ Work History ☐ JIST Card

Reference #4

Name _____

Address _____

City, State, ZIP _____

Phone (h) _____ Phone (w) _____

Time known _____ Relationship _____

Occupation _____ Company _____

Has: ☐ Resume ☐ Work History ☐ JIST Card

JOB-RELATED PERSONAL INFORMATION

Position Desired _____

Second Choice _____

Salary Desired _____

Date Available _____ Preferred Hours _____

Willing to Work Weekends (____ Yes ____ No); Holidays (____ Yes ____ No);

Overtime (____ Yes ____ No)

Willing to Relocate to _____
_____

Certifications, Registrations, Licenses:

Type _____ Date _____

Type _____ Date _____

Driver's License # _____ Type _____

Professional Organizations (currently member):

Name _____ Office _____

Name _____ Office _____

Hobbies, Interests, Leisure Activities _____
_____
_____

Successes and Achievements _____
_____
_____

Transferable Skills	Self-Management Skills
_____	_____
_____	_____
_____	_____
_____	_____
_____	_____
_____	_____
_____	_____
_____	_____
_____	_____
_____	_____

& TRAINING

Fields of Study and Special Courses	Number of Hours Completed	Diploma or Degree	Grade Point Average
major: minor:			
major: minor:			
major: minor:			
major: minor:			
major: minor:			
Location:			
8 9 10 11	12 13	14 15	16 16+

EDUCATION

School	Name of School and Complete Address	From		To		Full Time	Part Time
		mo.	yr.	mo.	yr.		
Primary							
Junior High							
Senior High							
College							
Other							
Other							
Other							
GED	Date Received:						

Circle the highest grade completed: 1   2   3   4   5   6   7

Types of Things Used on the Job (tools, machines, or equipment):

NJ L D

Creative Ideas (ideas that helped the company or made your job easier):

NJ L D

Other Duties and Special Responsibilities (be as specific as possible):

NJ L D

WORK EXPERIENCE MILITARY

Service Branch_____ From _____ To _____

Highest Rank Held _____ Service Number _____

Type of Work Performed _____

_____

Armed Forces Code _____ Honorable Discharge Y ☐ N ☐

If No Honorable Discharge, explain (discuss with instructor first)

_____

Vietnam Era Veteran Y ☐ N ☐ Registered with Selective Service Y ☐ N ☐

Service-related Disabilities: Y ☐ N ☐

If yes, explain _____

Commendations or Awards (if yes, explain) _____

_____

Reason for Leaving Military _____

_____

Types of Data/Information Used
(records kept, number, percentages, sales, etc.):

NJ L D

List "People Oriented" Duties/Responsibilities
(with co-workers, superiors, customers, etc.):

NJ L D

Types of Things Used on the Job (tools, machines, or equipment):

NJ L D

Creative Ideas (ideas that helped the company or made your job easier):

NJ L D

Other Duties and Special Responsibilities (be as specific as possible):

NJ L D

WORK EXPERIENCE   VOLUNTEER 1

Organization _____ Phone _____

Address _____

City _____ State _____ ZIP _____

Position/Title _____ Supervisor _____

Start Date _____ Leave Date _____ Days Missed _____

Reason for Leaving (must be positive) _____

_____

Supervisory Duties (if yes, explain) _____

_____

Promotion (if yes, explain)_____

_____

Commendations or Awards (if yes, explain) _____

_____

Types of Data/Information Used
(records kept, number, percentages, sales, etc.):

NJ L D

List "People Oriented" Duties/Responsibilities
(with co-workers, superiors, customers, etc.):

NJ L D

Types of Things Used on the Job (tools, machines, or equipment):

NJ L D

Creative Ideas (ideas that helped the company or made your job easier):

NJ L D

Other Duties and Special Responsibilities(be as specific as possible):

NJ L D

WORK EXPERIENCE   PAID EMPLOYMENT   JOB 4

Employer _____ Phone _____

Address _____

City _____ State _____ ZIP _____

Position/Title _____ Supervisor _____

Start Date _____ Leave Date _____ Start Salary _____ End Salary _____

Number of Days Missed _____ Explain _____

Reason for Leaving (must be positive) _____

_____

Supervisory Duties (if yes, explain) _____

_____

Merit Raises or Promotion (if yes, explain) _____

_____

Recommendations or Awards (if yes, explain) _____

_____

Commendations or Awards (if yes, explain) _____

_____

Types of Data/Information Used
(records kept, number, percentages, sales, etc.):

NJ L D

List "People Oriented" Duties/Responsibilities
(with co-workers, superiors, customers, etc.):

NJ L D

Types of Things Used on the Job (tools, machines, or equipment):

NJ L D

Creative Ideas (ideas that helped the company or made your job easier):

NJ L D

Other Duties and Special Responsibilities (be as specific as possible):

NJ L D

WORK EXPERIENCE   PAID EMPLOYMENT   JOB 3

Employer _____ Phone _____

Address _____

City _____ State _____ ZIP _____

Position/Title _____ Supervisor _____

Start Date _____ Leave Date _____ Start Salary _____ End Salary _____

Number of Days Missed _____ Explain _____

Reason for Leaving (must be positive) _____

_____

Supervisory Duties (if yes, explain) _____

_____

Merit Raises or Promotion (if yes, explain) _____

_____

Recommendations or Awards (if yes, explain) _____

_____

Commendations of Awards (if yes, explain) _____

_____

Types of Data/Information Used
(records kept, number, percentages, sales, etc.):

NJ L D

List "People Oriented" Duties/Responsibilities
(with co-workers, superiors, customers, etc.):

NJ L D

Types of Things Used on the Job (tools, machines, or equipment):

NJ L D

Creative Ideas (ideas that helped the company or made your job easier):

NJ L D

Other Duties and Special Responsibilities (be as specific as possible):

NJ L D

WORK EXPERIENCE   PAID EMPLOYMENT   JOB 2

Employer _____ Phone _____

Address _____

City _____ State _____ ZIP _____

Position/Title _____ Supervisor _____

Start Date _____ Leave Date _____ Start Salary _____ End Salary _____

Number of Days Missed _____ Explain _____

Reason for Leaving (must be positive) _____

_____

Supervisory Duties (if yes, explain) _____

_____

Merit Raises or Promotion (if yes, explain) _____

_____

Recommendations or Awards (if yes, explain) _____

_____

Commendations or Awards (if yes, explain) _____

_____

Types of Data/Information Used
(records kept, number, percentages, sales, etc.):

NJ L D

List "People Oriented" Duties/Responsibilities
(with co-workers, superiors, customers, etc.):

NJ L D

Types of Things Used on the Job (tools, machines, or equipment):

NJ L D

Creative Ideas (ideas that helped the company or made your job easier):

NJ L D

Other Duties and Special Responsibilities (be as specific as possible):

NJ L D

WORK EXPERIENCE   PAID EMPLOYMENT   JOB 1

Employer _____ Phone _____

Address _____

City _____ State _____ ZIP _____

Position/Title _____ Supervisor _____

Start Date _____ Leave Date _____ Start Salary _____ End Salary _____

Number of Days Missed _____ Explain _____

Reason for Leaving (must be positive) _____

_____

Supervisory Duties (if yes, explain) _____

_____

Merit Raises or Promotion (if yes, explain) _____

_____

Recommendations or Awards (if yes, explain) _____

_____

Commendations or Awards (if yes, explain) _____

_____

Types of Data/Information Used
(records kept, number, percentages, sales, etc.):

NJ L D

List "People Oriented" Duties/Responsibilities
(with co-workers, superiors, customers, etc.):

NJ L D

PERSONAL IDENTIFICATION

Name _____

Social Security Number _____

Present Address _____

_____

Length of Time Lived at Present Address _____

Previous Address _____

_____

Length of Time at Previous Address _____

Telephone (home) _____ (other) _____

Height _____ ft. _____ in. Weight _____ lbs.

Eye Color _____ Hair Color _____

Date of Birth (month) _____ (day) _____ (year) _____

Place of Birth (city) _____ (state) _____

U.S. Citizen? _____ Visa (number) _____ (type) _____

Marital Status _____

In Case of Emergency, Notify:

    Name _____

    Relationship _____ _____

    Address _____

    Phone Number _____

Physician's Name _____

    Address _____

    Phone Number _____

Date of Most Recent Physical Examination _____

Are you under a doctor's care, or taking medication? Explain. _____

_____

Do you have any physical or medical restrictions? Explain. _____

_____

Will the restrictions/medications affect your job performance? Explain.

_____

_____